For God hath not given us
the spirit of fear; but of
power, and of love, and of a
sound mind.

II Timothy 1:7

ALBERT GUÉRARD

Bottle in the Sea

HARVARD UNIVERSITY PRESS

CAMBRIDGE, MASS.: 1 9 5 4

To Brandeis University

IN GRATEFUL MEMORY

OF A LONG INDIAN SUMMER

By Albert Guérard

Contents

Contents

PART I

Thought

A DISCOURSE ON METHOD

"Come now, and let
us reason together,"
saith the Lord.
                Isaiah 1:18

CHAPTER I

Prove all things

The natural language of the poet is symbol, the natural language of the prophet is passion, the natural language of the mystic is silence. I, a teacher, must be satisfied with plain rational discourse. I am aware that there are worlds beyond speech and beyond sense. But when I put my thoughts on paper, I am condemned to abide within the limits of the intelligible. I know twilight when I reach it; and beyond that, I know the dark.

I define myself as "a rationalist — within reason." This is no idle jest. It means, first of all, that there are domains beyond reason, in which the laws of thought lose their validity. Pascal said: "The heart has reasons of its own, which reason cannot fathom," and to "the heart," or sentiment, we might add instinct, imagination, ecstasy. It implies also that even in the intellectual sphere reason is not identical with formal logic. Here our spokesman is Molière. His Chrysale, a sturdy bourgeois, complains that his whole household is crazed with reasoning, and that "reasoning drives reason away." Molière's reason, classical reason, was no scholastic scaffolding. It meant *reasonableness*, i.e., balance, moderation, sympathy, practical sense; even, in homeopathic doses at any rate, a wholesome respect for custom and public opinion. Reasoning is rectilinear, rigid, ruthless; reasonableness is sinuous, many-sided, finely shaded. Montaigne was a master of reasonableness; Robespierre, of reasoning. On the one hand, the living man, "fluctuating and diverse"; on the other, the robot of thought, the animated theorem. Montaigne's weapon was the smile of urbane kindly irony; Robespierre's, the guillotine. The reasonableness of the Lord rebuked with gentle mockery the fierce logical anger of Jonah.

But prophet, poet, lover, mystic, and modest rationalist, although they move on different planes, have one great duty in common: to preserve their integrity. For all of them, the first and greatest commandment is: "Thou shalt not pretend, least of all to thyself." There is some hope for the man who seeks to deceive others: if exposed, he has to acknowledge the error of his ways. But a soul which cannot discriminate between deception, make-believe, will-to-believe, belief and knowledge is in danger of hell-fire.

Through the fifty years of my teaching career, I have constantly quoted to my students Hans Christian Andersen's parable, *The Emperor's New Clothes*. Swindlers claimed to weave garments invisible to the eyes of fools; and the whole court, including the Emperor, professed to be delighted with their elusive fabric. In real life, the swindlers are far more plausible and far more insidious than in the tale. Their names are Authority, Orthodoxy, Loyalty, Tradition, Common Sense. To accept the *mores* is morality; to dissent is sin. For aeons, all right-minded men knew that the sun revolved round the earth; for ages, it was common knowledge that the gods revealed their will through omens, portents, and oracles, and that they demanded blood sacrifices. A century ago, honest Americans could still believe that slavery was in accord with God's holy ordinance. Only yesterday, it was right and proper to torture the feet of Chinese women. At this very moment, war as an instrument of national policy, and public service for private gain are accepted without a qualm by earnest and intelligent men. Whoever challenged such well-established truths was branded as insane or subversive, in rebellion against all laws human and divine. It takes a genius or a child spontaneously to exclaim: "Why, the Emperor has no clothes on at all!" For most of us, this victory of simplicity cannot be achieved without a sustained and painful effort. And, on the practical plane, the reward is dubious: there are jails for those who cannot see the Emperor's clothes.

There can be no honesty of thought without a conscientious, i.e., a fearless critique of every established opinion, however hoary and massive it may seem. This is not sheer iconoclasticism, nor an irresponsible desire to smash the idols of the common herd and of the elder generation: it is the initial step in every philosophy, from Socrates to Jean-Paul Sartre; it might even be called the essence of all philosophy, an essence which philosophical *systems* do not invariably preserve. Many philosophers strive first of all to consolidate orthodoxies, to justify the *recognized* ways of God to man. Hegel, apostle of liberty and reason, led free and rational minds to the worship of the Prussian state.

The boldest thinkers attempt to create a new and final orthodoxy which will silence doubt for ever. It will be a recurring theme in this book that all systems, political, economic, religious, and aesthetic, are intricate devices for arresting the flow of thought. Once you accept St. Thomas Aquinas, Auguste Comte, or Karl Marx, all your troubles are at an end. Science has but lately abandoned the hope of reaching immutable verities: the laws of gravitation, and above all the laws of evolution, are constantly open to scrutiny, challenge, revision, recall. There may be eternal truths: but the shadows of those truths perceptible to the human mind are forever in the making. And in this book I propose to speak in purely human terms.

I could discuss this conception of the unremitting challenge on the sole basis of my own experience: this is a testimony, not a treatise. It is a fact that although I was exposed in my adolescence to Socrates, Kant, and Herbert Spencer, it was not they who created the crisis in my thought. My teacher was the Dreyfus Affair. Circumstances compelled me, when I was still in my teens, to question the sacred character of the Flag, the Army, the Nation, the State, the Law, the Masses (*vox populi*), and even the Church. Their authorized representatives strove desperately to impede justice; and justice prevailed. We were then called in derision the *Intellectuals*; but we were first of all the *Believers*. We rationalized our passions — holy, I still claim — into a method. Orthodox Dreyfusism on the contrary became a system, and, on the morrow of victory, a form of government. For the quest of justice and truth, it substituted anticlericalism; for free thought, pseudo-scientific materialism;

for the love of liberty, Jacobinism. When our ideals appeared in the uncouth guise of Little Father Combes [1] many of us recoiled. But we did not recant: even through the dinginess of *petit bourgeois* politics, a few were still clutching the inviolable shade.

This I have said [2] and need not repeat at length. I am seeking a common denominator between myself and my unknown reader: my adolescent indignation, nearly sixty years ago, would not serve that purpose very well. To light the way in our quest, Spinoza and Kant would be admirable beacons. I chose René Descartes as a guide, because he deliberately appealed to the thoughtful general public. He did not seek refuge in a jungle of technicalities, nor escape into the impalpable inane of abstractions. His greatness and his limitations are plainly revealed. We can shrug away much of his science, and we shall pick obvious flaws in his would-be Euclidian reasoning. Still, he gave a great example and opened a perilous path.

A few years ago, in a symposium, I was requested to discuss "Descartes and French Literature," and my opening statement was: "If literature were mere literature, the place of Descartes in that pleasant realm, either as a performer or as an influence, would be very small indeed; and this paper [3] might emulate the masterly brevity, praised by Dr. Samuel Johnson, of the chapter on *Snakes in Iceland.*" René Descartes wrote his *Discourse on Method* in French, and we are told that this marked the emancipation of the vernacular, since hitherto all philosophical treatises had been written in Latin. But we must not forget that nearly a century before Calvin had translated his *Institutes of the Christian Religion* into the vulgar tongue, and that there was much philosophy, in a very legitimate sense of the word, in Montaigne's *Essays* — a breviary *of savoir-vivre* and *savoir-mourir*, the only *know-how* that matters. As an artist, Descartes does not rank very high. There are a few crisp and telling sen-

---

[1] Emile Combes, 1835–1921. Premier of France, 1902–1905; Minister of State in the Cabinet of Sacred (National) Union, 1914.
[2] In *Personal Equation* (New York, 1948), pp. 114–140.
[3] *Pacific Spectator*, Summer 1951.

tences in the autobiographical parts of the *Discourse;* but on the whole his style, if not leaden, is solid cast-iron. A few years later, Pascal and Bossuet were to prove that the most searching and the most cogent thought could be expressed in language of living majesty. They belong to literature, without any suspicion of would-be elegance or clever frivolity. Descartes does not enter the temple.

The problem changes altogether if we consider literature as one of the essential components of culture, inseparable from the rest. Then we find that the truly great books are those which wrestle with great problems, far more vital than mere technicalities or mere entertainment. Such books mirror the hope, the dread, the striving of many minds, of an age, of a nation, of humanity at large. In this deeper sense, all *sacred* books belong to literature; and the Bible of Mankind must include the *Discourse on Method.*

Consider a few dates. In 1635, the French Academy, pre-existing as a club of gentlemen interested in good language, assumes formal organization, and is acknowledged as an authority. In 1636, Paris is swept with enthusiasm by Corneille's first masterpiece, *Le Cid.* The Hôtel de Rambouillet is attempting to enforce a code of good manners. Malherbe and Guez de Balzac have disciplined poetry and prose. Above them all stands Richelieu, curbing feudal chaos with a hand of steel. Such is the moment when the *Discourse* appears.

Evidently Descartes's method neither was the cause of these parallel activities, nor was it determined by them. In every domain we discover the same spirit: *a craving for intelligent order.* At the end of the sixteenth century, France had faced utter dissolution. The Renaissance, that magnificent release of human energy, had led to moral anarchy and the splendid ruffianism of a Cesare Borgia. The Reformation, at first a glorious hope like the Renaissance, then a sharp reaction against its paganism, had caused spiritual disruption, and the outbreak of ferocious, most un-Christian wars. The long quarrel of the Guises and the Bourbons, under the cloak of religious differences, recalled the rivalry of Armagnacs and Bourguignons during the Hundred Years' War, itself a relapse into the brutal confusion of the Dark Ages. France had escaped, through the smiling, shrewd, persistent opportunism of Henry IV. But Henry, a crowned Montaigne, was himself the product of a troublous time. Skeptical at heart, with a touch of kindly cynicism, he could offer only a temporary solution: appeasement, not peace. Chaos was still menacing, exactly as chaos is threatening to engulf us today.

It was the greatness of classical France that she would not capitulate to chaos. Twice at least Germany, in the heyday of the Romantic school and in the debased romanticism of the Nazis, deliberately flung herself into the *Abgrund*, as an escape from moral responsibility, just as Pirandello's Henry IV sought refuge in madness; and that spiritual suicide was extolled as a sign of profundity. Out of the tragic welter, France sought to evolve order. The most signal victory in this great campaign for the dignity of discipline was the *Discourse on Method*; and for us today the same kind of mental effort, earnest, sustained, clear-eyed, is again the path of salvation.

The Cartesian victory was the triumph, not of abstract intelligence, but of the heroic will. What most impresses us with the men and the women of that age is their indomitable courage. Even the most obvious kind of bodily courage: it is the age of d'Artagnan and Cyrano, whose rapiers were as swift and keen as their wits. There was a touch of willful braggadocio about them, if you like, as there was about Corneille, their contemporary. But there is firmness of thought under the bluster. The heroes of Corneille do not merely rant, they reason; and in the swashbuckler Cyrano, there was a thinker, bold and free. The great Cardinal-Duke himself did not merely have the moustaches and the pointed beard of a cavalier: he appeared booted and cuirassed before the ramparts of La Rochelle. This musketeer element is present in our hero of pure thought, Descartes. At twenty-five, in West Frisia, threatened by a scoundrelly crew of ferrymen, he held them in respect at the point of the sword. A few years later, he fought a duel with a rival, under the eyes of the lady they were seeking to win. It is curious but not ab-

surd that young Descartes should have selected, not the cloister
or the study, but the army, and that he should have been for
years, like Cyrano, a gentleman-adventurer. For them, camp
life did not stifle philosophy. The military mind in its purity
refuses to acknowledge thought altogether: "Theirs not to reason
why," and ignoring it, leaves it free. A businessman, a minister
of the gospel, a doctor, a teacher, have to think of many things:
a soldier does not have to think at all. In the case of Descartes
as in the case of Alfred de Vigny, freedom *from* thought led to
freedom *of* thought. Neither, I must add, reached high rank
in the service.[4]

I insist that the first step in the growth of Descartes's philosophy was an act of the will, not of reflection. Reflection was the
fruit, not the seed. Here Descartes followed one of the rules
of his provisional code of action: decide, at random if need be,
and then go right ahead. For, he argues, if you are lost in a
forest, it is better to go the longest and hardest way out than
to stand still and moan, run in circles, or dash into twenty different paths, only to abandon them after a few steps. Descartes
the man of decision is thus the exact opposite of Hamlet: perhaps not Shakespeare's Hamlet, who like Shakespeare remains
an enigma, but the Hamlet that Goethe and Coleridge have impressed upon the world.

Strictly, Descartes should have said: "I will, therefore I am."
In the beginning is, not the Word or the Thought, but the Act.
Back of the Act (if it be an act indeed and not a mere reflex)
stands the Will; back of the Will, the Hope or Dread; and back
of the Hope or Dread stands the Pain. The key of life is suffering; no dynamic philosophy was ever evolved by contented cows;
and there is no steadfast bliss except in Nirvana.

Think your way through your pain to nobler levels of pain.
And thinking must start with a decision. Descartes's doubt was
not a datum of experience: he made himself doubt, and he
made himself think his way out of his doubt. In this, his attitude

---

[4] Among soldiers who evinced originality of thought, we might mention Vauvenargues, Choderlos de Laclos (a high-ranking *liaison* officer),
and Stendhal.

was purely Cornelian. It is a commonplace that the great characters in Corneille are not the servants of duty, but the heroes — splendidly sinister at times — of inflexible will. This is manifest in Corneille's earliest tragedy, still stiff and bombastic like a Senecan drama, *Medea*. It extols the self-reliance of the individual soul, deprived of all earthly support:

> Your country abhors you, your spouse is faithless:
> In such a dire plight, what remains to you?
>   Myself.
> Myself alone, and that suffices.

Myself alone, and that suffices. It is the same movement by which Descartes sweeps aside all reassuring authorities: institutions, traditions, and even our own senses, which might be a mystification played upon us by a deity with a perverse sense of humor. In this total devastation of the intellectual universe, "what remains to you? — Myself." "Never to accept a thing as true unless it appears *to me* clearly and evidently to be such." This, manifestly, is the attitude of all the great heroes of thought, rebels, prophets, and founders. They speak directly, as having authority, and not as the scribes. It is the attitude of Joan of Arc refusing to submit the validity of her visions to the verdict of the Church; it is the attitude of Luther at the Diet of Worms: "So help me God, I cannot otherwise."

At this stage, Descartes goes beyond the subjectivism, the egocentricity of the Romanticists: he has reached the point of pure solipsism. His own existence alone is a fact: the rest of the world he spins out of his own reason, and the evidence for it is only at second hand.

Like all radical doctrines, solipsism is at the same time irrefutable and futile. So far as I know, I may be alone in the world; but I am none the less conscious of conflicts, obstacles, and friendly support. These I personify into separate beings, just as the primitives personify the forces of nature, or as the theists personify the universe. It is perfectly possible that my friends, my enemies, my sources of pain and delight, are all within me, part of that teeming, snarling ménagerie which I call I. Possibly life is a dream, as Calderón and so many others would have it; or more profoundly, with Grillparzer, the dream, the inner mental process, is a life. Yes, there are dreams within dreams; some consistent, some fluid; some fugitive, some enduring; some that obey, some that elude our control. Nothing proves that if I were to cease dreaming the whole universe — *my* universe — would not vanish, leaving not a rack behind. But, all this granted, what odds does it make? In my solipsistic world, I have to live as though a certain nucleus of consciousness had a separate existence, and had to win or fight its way among similar nuclei. I could conceive of an Ego so harmonious, so absolute, that it would annihilate all recalcitrant sub-centers. Such an Ego would be conscious only of its own unity and unicity. The god of the metaphysicians is such an Ego. The God of the believers is not. He made others — angels of light, angels of darkness, and those uneasy creatures of twilight, men — in order to escape from the infinite boredom of a solipsistic universe.

Solipsism cannot be dismissed as an absurdity: it is the metaphysical foundation, or perhaps the metaphysical caricature, of radical individualism. The rugged self-reliance preached by Herbert Spencer, Ibsen, and Herbert Hoover is fully justified only if others do not count; and they must count, if they exist at all. If we acknowledge that there are others, that we must find ourselves in a plural world, then "devil take the hindmost" becomes rank selfishness. The presence of others creates a social atmosphere and social duties. Man is a sociable animal; he is bound to be to a large extent a socialist. Descartes took pains to refute solipsism, not very convincingly. The one decisive argument against it is not intellectual, but moral. The man who lives in a "private universe" is, literally, a monster; and, etymologically, an idiot.

That sweeping aside of all established fences is Descartes's systematic doubt, the core of his method, and the lesson we need more imperiously than ever today. Tennyson said, with his middle-road wisdom (if only we could recover it!),

> There lives more faith in honest doubt,
> Believe me, than in half the creeds.

Had he gone further, beyond the bournes of Victorian propriety, he would have rejoined Descartes and said: "No faith is valid unless it has passed through the crucible of doubt." *Prove*, that is to say, try or test, all things. God has no need of our delusions or of our lies. If they be delusions or lies, they are obstacles, and not guides.

I have repeatedly quoted the experience of Don Quixote, equipping himself for his chivalrous quest. He made a helmet out of pasteboard, and at the first try smashed it with his sword. Then, nothing daunted, he made himself a second helmet, likewise out of pasteboard, and prudently refrained from putting it to the test. That is why he was Don Quixote, the great delusionist: he refused to doubt, when doubt would have been sanity. "Help thou mine unbelief": not dispel or destroy, but help, that is to say guide, enlighten, sustain my unbelief, because unbelief is the only safe path toward the true light. Uncritical belief follows every will-o'-the-wisp: there are strange creeds in Los Angeles. Many nineteenth-century writers wailed, and at times whined, over their doubt, a corrosive force destroying the integrity of their thought: Amiel's *Journal* is an interminable dirge over his shattered faith. There is no trace of such despair in Descartes. His doubt was triumphant even before it had reached its goal. For he had faith in his own doubt, that is to say in himself.

There are at least three great forms of doubt, and all three are excellently illustrated in French literature. Their intellectual content, their spiritual resonance, are different. The first is Montaigne's. It is not the very foundation of his thought, for he was a stoic at heart. But in an age rent asunder by rival fanaticisms, doubt was the one path of return to sanity. Montaigne revels in his own doubt. His *Apology for Raymond de Sebonde* is a spirited, almost exulting catalogue of all the diversities, conflicts, and absurdities of human opinions. In this confusion, "doubt is a soft pillow for a well-made head." But that doubt was not an end in itself. The lesson most pressing in Montaigne's days, as it is still in ours, was: "Do not take your opinions with such tragic earnestness as to be ready, for their sake, to roast your fellow-men alive." Anger is a weakness; and righteous anger is a deadly sin.

There is deep seriousness in Montaigne; but, at the exact point where it is focused for us, his skepticism is inseparable from a smile and a shrug. "What do I know? And, moreover, what do I care?" It is the amiable tolerant skepticism of The Book of Jonah, of its modern version *The Vision of Babouc*, of Renan in his last phase, and of Renan's disciple, Abbé Jérôme Coignard. Within its field, it is not to be despised. But there is nothing of the kind in Descartes. He is no jesting Pilate. His *"Que sçais-je?"* is uttered in a different tone.

There is a third, and poetically a greater doubt, which is not self-willed like Descartes's and not self-satisfied like Montaigne's. It is that of Pascal. That doubt is inseparable from anguish: the torment of a noble soul for whom the sufferings of the world are a presumption of mysterious guilt. Pascal seeks with groaning: *"chercher en gémissant,"* as Descartes seeks with confidence and quiet joy. For Pascal, doubt is not the indispensable and trusted instrument, but the enemy. Perhaps he was closer to Descartes than he was ready to confess. He had not integrated doubt as a necessary process of his faith, but he was too superbly honest to discard doubt. His *Apology for the Christian Religion* was to be a life-and-death wrestling with doubt, as a formidable and worthy enemy. At times, he almost despaired, and was ready to accept an opiate: "Practise, tell your beads: it will stupefy you," and so alleviate the malady of thought. But his central argument is Cartesian: in the dark forest, choose your path and follow it with determination. That choice, not necessarily reasonable, perhaps above reason, perhaps below, is what he calls his *wager*: *"Les jeux sont faits: rien ne va plus."*

In Descartes, there is no smile and no anguish: only a deep and calm gravity. By doubting, he becomes more purely himself; he rises above prejudices and passions; he is conscious of his very essence. Elliptically: "I doubt, therefore I am." This reaching unafraid to the very bedrock of his thought is an act of daring which, in its purity, is unexampled; but, I repeat, it is in harmony with the spirit of his time. Descartes is a Nico-

mède[5] defying and deriding even the might of Rome. He
achieves quietly, without bluster, what Pascal was to express in
the noblest passage in all French literature: "Man is but a reed,
the frailest in Nature; but he is a thinking reed. He is greater
than the material universe that crushes him, because he knows
that he is crushed." No Titanic defiance: a steadfast assurance
of spiritual dignity.

In Voltaire, there was a blend of Montaigne and Descartes.
The Pascal element was hidden, but not wholly lacking: read
the *Poem on the Lisbon Disaster.* We find the same Cartesian-
Cornelian courage in Alfred de Vigny, but this time with a dark
inner glow which reminds us of Pascal. As Descartes undertook
the great voyage to the end of the night, so did Vigny; but it was
the moral night, not the intellectual. He rejected all conventional comforts as Descartes had swept aside all traditional authorities. He found no joy in Nature, in the love of Delilah, in
God Himself, the God of eternal silence. He yearned for their
companionship, but he had to face their implacable indifference. For the just and proud man, to groan, to weep, to pray
are equal in cowardice. But Vigny does not, like Schopenhauer
and Leconte de Lisle, rejoice in his own pessimism. He too
reaches bedrock; and like Descartes, like Pascal, he finds his
strength and his dignity in thought. He does not yield to the dark
forces: he fights his way through them into the light. Suffering
ennobles, and the key to salvation is tender and active pity, not
for one's self, but for one's fellow-sufferers. Then, all idols
swept aside, passions transcended, catharsis attained, Vigny
closes with a hymn to the Pure Spirit, the God of Ideas, the God
of Descartes.

We find the same movement again in the modern French
existentialists. (I hate the word, and its futile pedantry.) They
face the fact, which Descartes and Hegel had not reached, that
this world does not obey the norms of our reason. Humanly
speaking, the universe is absurd. It is indifferent: to curse it as
hostile would be the merest pathetic fallacy. But by calling it

[5] In Corneille's tragedy *Nicomède*, which, by the way, deserves to be
better known.

absurd, we affirm a verity which stands apart from, and above, the chaos of the apparent cosmos. The man who has the courage to reflect creates a little zone of light and order in the all-pervading murk. That conviction is found in Sartre, and even more lucidly in Camus, as it is in Descartes, Pascal, Vigny. That is why they could not capitulate, as did Céline and Montherlant, to the forces of nihilism. All was lost, but they found in themselves, and in themselves alone, the power to resist. And their resistance was not a blind instinct, like the rage of an animal caught in a trap: it was founded on reason. What they were defending against the absurd was the dignity of thought, which is the whole dignity of man.

CHAPTER II

Above compromise

Freedom is inherent in thought. The inorganic world is not free; creatures of instincts and reflexes are not free; robots are not free; men swayed unthinkingly by mass prejudices are not free. And the test of freedom is the right to challenge. This, to my mind, is the essence of Cartesianism. It is not the whole of René Descartes in his rich personality.

No man of flesh, not even a Robespierre, can be an incarnated theorem; none, not even a Trotsky or a de Gaulle, can be a pure act of the will. Our supreme logician was of contradictions all compact. I have presented him as a hero of thought: he had, in abundance, his cautious streaks. In his provisional code, he decided to follow scrupulously the customs, the laws, and the faith of his age and country. Above all, he wanted no quarrel with the Church, and to that effect he took precautions which Bossuet himself was to declare excessive. That, however, was fully half a century after the event: when Descartes was writing, the Galileo case was fresh in people's minds. Descartes was heroic, but he elected to stop short of martyrdom. What is the use of martyrdom? It cannot be accepted as evidence: fools are willing and eager to suffer for their delusions. Why should the wise expose themselves to indignities, perhaps to death, in order to maintain that the world is more than six thousand years old? What Descartes wanted to save was the *method*, which, he firmly believed, would inevitably bring about the triumph of truth. A Victor Hugo, fond of flamboyant attitudes (why should not a noble soul rejoice in a scarlet cloak?) could claim: "If there be one only who dares to resist, I shall be that one." We feel that Descartes and Goethe were too self-possessed and too shrewd for such defiance. They would have signed any loyalty oath required of them. Perhaps with an inward smile or an imperceptible shrug: "On your plane, I promise I shall not interfere with your idols; on my own plane, I am free." Through this prudence, Descartes truly belonged to the age of reasonableness.[1] There was in him no taint of Byronic defiance.

This moderation of the great radical raises a problem so complex that I for one cannot discern any hard and fast solution, binding upon all men under all possible circumstances, the problem of compromise. Compromise has been extolled as the great Anglo-Saxon contribution to politics, philosophy and religion; it is favorably contrasted with the unswerving logic of the alleged "Latin" mind; as though the Italians, noted for their mastery of *combinazioni*, were not the original "Latins"! By virtue of compromise, we are told, England always manages to "muddle through somehow." I am weary of pointing out that if England muddles into disaster, as under Neville Chamberlain, she has to redeem herself through decision, will-power, clear-eyed efficiency, as under Winston Churchill. There is no saving grace in confusion, and no virtue in capitulation; and compromise, as distinct from delicate and equitable adjustment, is both confusion and capitulation. It means condoning — out of weariness or indifference, for fear of worse evils, in hope of some greater good — that which our conscience denounces as evil.

There is a trick of thought which, in my *Personal Equation*, I have called the *Excelsior!* fallacy. First assert your ideal in the most absolute terms; carry "the banner with the strange device" even unto death; hitch your wagon to a star; uphold the Eternal Verities; spurn every path that strays from the will of the Lord. Then, when you have reached a comfortable glow of self-right-

---

[1] Rabelais offered the same blend of intellectual courage and worldly prudence when he averred that he would maintain his opinions *up to* the fire but not *into* the fire: *"jusqu'au feu — exclusivement."* So did Mirabeau when he proudly declared: "We are here by the will of the people, and shall not yield *except to the force of bayonets.*" If you refuse to acknowledge the bayonets as a valid *ultima ratio*, you would be wise to rob them of their prey. Then you may live to see bayonets placed at the service of reason.

eousness, turn sharply round: "All this is very beautiful indeed; we are proud to affirm our faith in it; but of course it will not work, and therefore it does not make sense. We have to deal, not with golden dreams, but with hard facts." In terms of current politics, we find men who denounce indignantly the materialism of the Marxians, yet consider idealism as the most damning political sin; champions of liberty who unblushingly seek the alliance of Chiang Kai-shek and Franco; professed Christians who sneer at *do-gooders*. To the rest of the world, this ambivalence looks embarrassingly like hypocrisy.

The immorality of such "deals" is manifest. As a student of history, I very much doubt even their earthly wisdom. There is nothing to be gained by pretending that a moral defeat is a moral victory; or by believing that somehow evil is transmuted into good, if only our interests are promoted. Such interests will be found as a rule to be personal, local, transient. They may enable us to win a contract, a law suit, an election, a battle: they cannot serve as a foundation for a sane and self-respecting life. Between general and permanent interests on the one hand and principles on the other, I can see no conflict. Rather I believe that, on the human plane, they are identical. No valid principle will lead a sound community into disaster. If disaster does occur, not as a mere physical catastrophe, but as the ineluctable consequence of thought and deed, then the principle was false and the community diseased.

Let me offer an historical example. At the time of the French Revolution, some anti-slavery orator, filled with the spirit of the Rights of Man, exclaimed: "Perish the colonies, rather than a principle!" For generations, these words were held up to ridicule, as the acme of hollow suicidal radicalism. Yet it was not because slavery was abolished that France ultimately lost Haiti: it was because the realist, Napoleon, attempted to restore it. Today colonialism, in the sense of imperial domination, is doomed as manifestly contrary to the democratic faith. And without qualms, indeed with a virtuous glow, we repeat: "Perish the *French* colonies, rather than a principle!"

Between radicalism — here in the sense of crude, unyielding, fanatical advocacy of abstract principles — and craven dishonest capitulation, it is not impossible to imagine a *via media* which itself is not a compromise. It is the path of *reasonableness*. That path is traced by reason in the first place, that is to say by a careful application of the mind; but it is not determined by rudimentary logic. The man who can see nothing but intense black and flawless white had better consult an ophthalmologist. Scrupulous and precise thinking — and any other kind is but a caricature — leads, much as we hate the term, to *casuistry*, the close examination of particular cases in their diversity and in their complexity. It is a law of nature that water flows down; but water does not flow quite in the same way in a pool and in a cataract; apart from the fact that external factors — the moon, the wind, a pump — may for a while force water upward. It is highly probable that the laws of society are far more subtle than the laws of nature; they may even be of a totally different character.

What I am attempting to define is the judicial process. A judge is inevitably a *casuist*. He is more than a rough computing machine, more even than the finest achievements of cybernetics. He must weigh and appraise the material facts, all the relevant facts, and the competent relations between these facts. He cannot accept any crude fact, uncritically, as decisive evidence. This scrupulous weighing requires intellectual gifts, thorough training, and a steadfast purpose. That is why, among men equally versed in the letter of the law, some judges are great, some are merely good, and many are indifferent. Through the intricate maze of circumstances, the judge must be guided by the law, and his mind must follow rational processes. No judge, unless his name be Bridlegoose, will hand out decisions on a hunch or a throw of the dice. No judge will assert the wisdom of "muddling through somehow": muddling is his first enemy. As for the "realists," who on the bench make deals between their convictions and the pressure of passions or interests, they are only masquerading as judges. The judicial mind is essentially rational, but not dogmatically rationalistic. Reason — the conscious, disciplined intellect — is not the path itself, but a guiding light; and that light, however clear, does not plunge very far into the encircling wilderness.

Descartes, in his own life, evinced cautious *reasonableness*, not the heroic folly of a Polyeucte, a nihilist, a firebrand. As a result, he was able to propound openly, in the vernacular, the most subversive of all doctrines, and yet escape persecution. Prudent in conduct, reckless in thought, his clear-cut personality offers an endless series of problems. The contradictions in him do not appear merely between the theoretical and the practical aspects of his life and thought: those which exist on the purely intellectual plane are striking enough. His opening act, determined doubt, is impressive; but all too soon he leaves doubt behind and reaches the self-evidence which destroys the possibility of further doubt. So he propounds absolute truths in his turn; but he is saved from the dogmatism that would naturally follow through the pragmatic notion of *common sense*. The three key thoughts of the Cartesian method — doubt, self-evidence, and general consent — are skillfully hammered together; they are not intimately welded, and the seams remain like scars.

I feel confident that Descartes's doubt was sincere, not a mere rhetorical device. But he was too eager to enter the realm of mathematical certitude. For all his courage, he sought refuge too soon. Before you challenge a prejudice, you have to recognize it as possibly a prejudice. Now both a prejudice and an axiom are unquestioned affirmations; and unquestioned is very easily made synonymous with unquestionable. Pascal was to write: "They say that habit is a second nature: what if nature were but a first habit?" Descartes accepted as primitive, as immediate data of consciousness, certain concepts which, to other thinkers, may appear as merely traditional.

Two illustrations will, I hope, suffice. The first is obvious and familiar enough: we in America officially hold certain truths to be *self-evident*, the first of which is that all men are created equal. In this blunt form, it is a paradox, if not a fallacy; self-evidence of this kind would not be accepted as evidence before any court. The second is more subtle. Descartes took it for granted that the notion of absolute perfection implied existence — the time-honored *ontological* argument. So if we conceive of a perfect being, such a being must exist: the ideal and the real are one. But, for one thing, we cannot "clearly and consistently" think of a perfect being; we can only deny imperfections. Thinking implies *delineating*, which means tracing boundaries, and *qualifying*, which excludes the qualities that are not affirmed. Both processes are incompatible with the notion of perfection in its absolute sense. They leave only the possibility of a limited, relative perfection: perfect is that which adequately fulfills a definite purpose. A truly perfect being, perfect absolutely, may be real, but he is not conceivable. Descartes had not anticipated Paul Valéry's profound, perhaps Buddhistic, conception that "existence is but a flaw in the purity of non-being," which is St. Anselm neatly turned inside out.

Beyond Descartes, but thanks to Descartes's example, we have reached the conception of incessant dialectical doubt, doubt lustily feeding on itself, doubt refusing to commit suicide. It is not doubt that ought to be provisional, but every partial "truth," transcended as soon as it is reached. Our thought is alive, growing, creative, dynamic. On the human plane, translated into human words, there are no immutable verities: there is an unceasing quest. This was most lucidly understood and most forcibly expressed by Lessing two centuries ago. The mind no longer in the making has reached the repose of death. Ye will *seek* the truth, and the *quest* shall make you free.

This brief excursion to the confines of metaphysics leads us back to our problem of compromise, or, better, adjustment. If, through the Cartesian approach or any other, we were in possession of the absolute truth, then fanaticism would be wisdom and virtue. There can be no toleration of manifest evil. I know that fire burns: I shall not permit a child to jump into the flames. And what is true of physical fire is true *a fortiori* of hell-fire. We can be saved from fanaticism only through the admission that perfection is beyond our reach and certitude beyond our ken. This relativity of all human knowledge and action does not preclude definite inquiry and definite endeavor. No man has any notion of his position in *absolute space*: the very question is absurd. But he is not lost: if he wants to go from New York to Boston, he has to solve spatial problems. But if we abandon the idea of absolute truths — the impregnable rock of religious dogma, the eternal verities of the philosophers, the ineluctable laws of scientific determinism — then we are no longer so ready to destroy everything that stands in our inflexible path.

This moderation, I must insist, is not founded on skepticism. We are not incapable of reaching definite results, and these "truths," although relative, may be of commanding and lasting value. Moderation does not condone moral indifference either. These "truths," if worth attaining, are worth defending. So long as we hold them to be truths, we have no right to barter them away. We can serve with a whole heart that which we know to be mortal: a lover, a country, a cause. Perhaps with deeper devotion because it is mortal. But these human truths, however valuable they may seem, are always open to challenge, to revision, to refinement, to refutation, to repeal. Only the quest is eternal.

This relativity of truth, translated into practical terms, means *pluralism*, the sole basis for a liberal society. Pascal poured contempt on those paltry human assertions which are "truths this side of the Pyrenees, and errors beyond." But the word *character* is accented differently in Spanish, English, and French: each form is *right* in its own language. For the monk, wealth is evil; for the capitalist — who may be a good Catholic and have a brother in a monastery — wealth is the reward of foresight, thrift, energy, public service. Some make the Nation an idol and the State an enemy; yet they would find it hard to sever the Nation from the State. In all such contradictions (I am not proposing to write another *Apology for Raymond de Sebonde*), the proper attitude is: "You may be justified within your own frame of reference. So long as your action does not interfere with mine, I have no right to object."

These contradictions do exist, not merely among neighbors, but within the individual himself. Every man is a pluralist: he lives in several worlds, interpenetrating, yet different. These worlds may clash: there are tragically divided souls. They may also reach a happy *modus vivendi*. A man may be a musician, a Democrat, a hardware dealer, a Congregationalist, and an ardent golfer. There is no necessary link between these various aspects of his personality; there is no irremediable conflict either. Our man will associate, on different planes, in ways that are profitable and pleasant, with other human beings whose complex formulae are different from his own. He may play chamber music with fellow musicians who are not Democrats, and discuss the problems of his trade with hardware men who are not Congregationalists. He rejects the rigid unity of totalitarianism, within himself, and among the groups to which he belongs. He is persuaded that each group is the right one for him, under present circumstances. He does not believe that his choice and lot are the only conceivable ones: we cannot all be hardware dealers.

It is my despair, on almost every page of this book, that I am compelled to reassert the obvious, when I should like to venture into the experimental. But the tritest lessons are still the most imperiously needed. We have learned, in this country at any rate, that national enmities are not "in the blood," but in the mind; that they are not sacred duties, but mental diseases which a healthy environment would cure; on these shores, a Pole, a German, a Frenchman, can be friends. We have learned that Jews, Catholics, Protestants, agnostics, could live side by side and work together. Yet *fellow-traveler* is still a term of reproach. In a liberal, i.e., in a pluralistic world, our plain duty is to find out how much we have in common with "the enemy," so as to restrict the area of enmity and expand the area of coöperation. In spite of *his* delusions, he too lives in a *pluriverse* which cannot be reduced to the petty definition of tribe, caste, sect, or party. At the core, he is not a Peruvian, or a Democrat, or a Mohammedan, or a Communist, "first, last, and all the time," but a man. The garments, well-fitting or grotesque, may be discarded: the man remains.

Thus every reliable guide — the judicial temper, the scientific method, the humanistic spirit, the teaching of Christ Himself — points to the same path: not to judge hastily, not to hate blindly, but, without anger or pride, to seek an equitable adjustment. The appeal of fanatical self-righteousness is great. It flatters vanity: we alone stand for unmitigated virtue. It sounds firm: "We shall never yield." Above all, it panders to our sloth: we no longer need to seek. We are in sole possession of the truth, world without end: *we rest satisfied.* The temptation is hard to resist; yet, unless it be conquered, our civilization will remain precarious, a castle of cards at the mercy of an angry breath.

Our method, therefore, should be first of all to spurn compromise, to reject any sacrifice of our intellectual and moral integrity: "never to accept anything as *right* unless we feel it, clearly and evidently, to be such." But at the same time, we must strive patiently for constant, finely shaded, dispassionate adjustment. What degree of truth is there in the contentions of our foes, either when they criticize our way of life, or when they extol their own? Can we devise some traffic signal that will enable currents of doctrine to cross without clashing? Is there no useful work that we can undertake in common? Can we stamp out fear and hatred from our hearts as degrading?

All this can be summed up in a word: *appeasement.* The fact that a weakling, Neville Chamberlain, misused the term many years ago as a mask for surrender does not destroy its validity. Without appeasement, there can be no peace: at best a sullen truce. Appeasement without compromise! Tenacity of purpose without fanaticism! When the first care of our leaders is to find out what is *right* with our opponents, then the cynical remark of Chancellor Oxenstjerna [2] will at last become obsolete, and we shall speed our sons on their grand tour with the words: "Go and see with how much wisdom the world is ruled."

---

[2] Count Axel Gustafsson Oxenstjerna (1583–1654), Chancellor of Sweden. The actual text ("*Quantilla sapientia regitur mundus!*") is uncertain; and even the ascription to Oxenstjerna. But it is good sense.

CHAPTER III

Common sense is not enough

We have noted some puzzling discrepancies, if not contradictions, between the principles of Descartes and some of his practical rules of conduct. No one can dispute his courage, yet he had a healthy measure of worldly prudence: perhaps the greatest explorer is not the most reckless, but the one who guards best against every contingency. We have noted also that after putting his trust in systematic doubt, he sought refuge at an early stage in the doubtful sanctuary of self-evidence, which precludes doubt. More striking still is the contrast between his proud solipsism: "Myself, alone, and that suffices!" and his appeal to, his reliance upon, public opinion.

There is nothing strange in his fighting the self-styled experts, the supercilious initiates, the pedants, entrenched in their citadels of formalized prejudices. Socrates had to do it, and so had Jesus: to break down the barriers of privilege is the first step in liberation. Descartes wrote in heavy but lucid nontechnical French, for the layman if not for the man in the street. He was the first of the great popularizers (*vulgarisateurs* in the strictly French sense): a distinguished line, and particularly Gallic, in which Pascal himself, and Renan, were to be his successors. He went so far as to include among his potential audience "even women": a revolutionary step, for the elaborate gallantry of the time had not yet broken down the prejudice against feminine brains: chivalry is the most delicate form of contempt. It is odd to think of the austere logician, mathematician, and physicist as a professor for society ladies: yet he had among his disciples Princess Elizabeth of Bohemia and Queen Christina of

Sweden. We might consider him as a forerunner of Trissotin in Molière's *Learned Ladies*; most decidedly of Fontenelle, whose *Chats on the Plurality of Inhabited Worlds* are masterpieces of drawingroom wit and courtesy; of Voltaire, who wrote his *Universal History* for Madame du Châtelet; of Bellac in Pailleron's *Le Monde où l'on s'ennuie*, the professor as society pet, a composite picture of many successful academic lecturers; even of Bergson, whose courses at the Collège de France were thronged with the aristocracy of birth and wealth.

This was not strictly an appeal to the people: I repeat that Descartes never wrote for the masses. But it was an appeal to *common sense*, "of all things the one most evenly divided among men." On the face of it, this assumption of Descartes's would justify democracy in the fallacious but indestructible meaning of the term: the quaint notion that the opinion of George F. Babbitt is as good as Einstein's. *Vox populi* would entice us into the bog of Rousseauism.

A very dangerous path: but Cartesianism is not unwary. Historically, the appeal to the common man is not unjustified. Not purely in the interests of the masses themselves: it might be argued that one shepherd is of more value than many sheep, and even that the shepherd knows best what is good for the sheep. But because the élites, however legitimate in their origin, inevitably stiffen in the defense of their vested interests. Every technical élite is bound to become pedantic; every social élite supercilious; every moral élite pharisaical. They are hard to dislodge: they have skill and power, and they occupy strategic positions. Against these the masses may well be used by a new élite as a battering ram. But once the gates are forced the battering ram becomes a cumbrous piece of junk.

Descartes turns to the common sense inborn in the common man, hoping to find there the verdict of the child in Andersen's tale: the robes of the learned are woven out of thin air. But does he reach the primitive unsophisticated truth? The minds of all men, gentle and simple, are thickly encrusted with prejudices. If the nobility, or the classical scholars, or the Calvinistic theologians, have their carapace of pride, the man in the street has his own blinding passions, all the more powerful for being rudimentary. Before we reach "the common sense of the common man," we have to remove — with delicate care, if we do not want to injure the brain in the process — layer after layer of superstition. We realize how prolonged, how difficult such an operation must be, when we remember that Descartes himself stopped short, and considered his own prejudices as unquestionable truths. The most vulgar "columns" are filled with assertions which to the uncritical appear self-evident. An exacting, unceasing effort is needed to make "common sense" fully available. In its purity — and purity is the result of refinement — common sense is the rarest commodity.

Descartes tells us that the most abstruse philosophical truths can be made intelligible to the common man, provided they be presented to him in proper sequence. He would contend that anybody can understand Einstein, if he is willing to take the trouble. Like most paradoxes, this bold affirmation hovers on the confines of the absurd. Yet Einstein himself might confirm it: he never claimed that he was bringing from the beyond a revelation inaccessible to human reason. The same fundamental processes are involved in elementary arithmetic and in the theory of relativity. The Cartesian assumption is not flatly contradicted by the results of modern aptitude tests: these merely measure differences in facility, which Descartes would not deny. He simply takes it for granted that no sane man is wholly impervious to elementary truths, mathematical or otherwise; and that the approach to higher truths can be made so gradual that at no point the common man will be irremediably baffled. The reverse hypothesis, that there are among normal intelligences radical differences in kind, and not merely in degree, is as difficult to prove as that of Descartes.

It is plain that the average man, even if he has the ability, has neither the patience nor the leisure to follow Einstein. The time may come when the path has been worn smooth: schoolgirls skip their merry way to summits unattainable to geniuses of the past; children could correct the astronomy of Dante, and college sophomores the physiology of Descartes. But the upward path, freely open to all, easy for later generations, is laborious for the pioneer. Descartes would never have suggested that the legislators of Tennessee were competent to pass upon the Darwinian hypothesis. They had common sense, I presume, and a healthy belief in "self-evident truths." But they did not know enough. Above all, they knew far too much that was not so.

Thus the intellectual democracy posited by Descartes is not wholly absurd. Common sense is not an actual body of knowledge. For knowledge is most decidedly not evenly distributed, even in these days of universal education. The mass of knowledge is shifting from day to day: we learn and unlearn at every step. Common sense is the power of connecting facts in your mind. In a rudimentary fashion, children, and even animals, possess that power. There is something *common* between the mental processes of a dog, who links the misdeed and the whip, and those of Newton, discovering the law which governs both the fall of an apple and the course of the heavenly bodies. It may be that such a sense is the same in all men, and that the obvious differences are due solely to unequal opportunities. The sense of a mechanic who fixes a carburetor is as good as the sense of the astrophysicist, the nuclear chemist, the microbiologist. Scale and complications do not alter the fundamental quality: the farmer who decides to go to law is not mentally inferior to the sovereign who decides to go to war. But if we committed ourselves to the Cartesian paradox of *even distribution*, we would have to reduce "sense" to a very tenuous abstraction. At every level, we find among men who enjoy the same opportunities some who judge more swiftly, more accurately, more comprehensively than others.

Consensus may be the result of common sense; it may also be the sum total of common prejudices. Common opinion blindly accepted is the reverse of common sense: it is the abdication of sense altogether. Pragmatists hope to extract *sense* out of *consensus*: sense would then confirm those things which have been accepted by all men, at all times and everywhere. This "catholic" definition would certainly not apply to the dogmas of any church or to the tenets of any political system. It is tempting to believe that the composite picture of two billion minds (mostly fools, Carlyle would growl) would give us the portrait of the normal man, the ideal man, that *Monsieur Tout-le-Monde* reputed to have more wit than Monsieur de Voltaire himself. I am not sure that this would be even roughly true, if we had indeed such a total composite picture. When we have two pictures striving to be different, as in an orthodox democracy, or in the schizophrenic world of today, the result is two caricatures glaring at each other: poor substitutes for the image of *Homo Sapiens*.

To sum up: there is a *sense*, perhaps not limited to mankind, and presumably common to all men, that enables us to establish connections between facts. These connections are ideas; and through an algebra of thought, we can proceed to trace relations between ideas, and between "ideas of ideas." Each man, to be truly human, must be credited with that capacity, and made responsible for its use. This is his certificate of citizenship.

But every man will soon find out that his own sense is in danger of being smothered by alleged consensus: the very fact that superstitions could arise proves that the sense of the race is far from infallible. It is the first duty of man to clean up his own instrument, so as to restore the purity of his own judgment: tradition and universal consent must both remain open to challenge.

Man must also realize that the world of thought is an elaborate structure. At every single step, it is for us to use our "sense": but we should be aware that there are innumerable steps. The simplicity of the child in Andersen's tale is not adequate to detect flaws in Marxian dialectics. Transparent honesty does not suffice; nor does the will to doubt; still less self-evidence, a mere resting place for the weary. We need the inquiring mind, and the critical [1] and the constructive. Only the union of all three will give validity to the Method.

[1] Under the critical, I include the experimental: an experiment is a test to meet reasonable doubt. A self-evident truth requires no experimental confirmation: it scorns experiment.

CHAPTER IV

ℭhe powers of darkness

𝔍n the domain of the "reason" and the "good sense" invoked by Descartes—man's capacity to observe facts, to establish connections between the facts observed—reason is sovereign. It cannot claim infallibility at any particular point; but it has the power of correcting its own mistakes. The intrusion of any other element would be irrelevant.

Suppose a bridge of a new design should collapse when barely completed. There might be pious souls to condemn the engineers for their sacrilegious attempt. Puny men posing as Titans, shallow materialists, they had failed to sacrifice a bullock to the local Spirit; and that Spirit, in his anger, snapped asunder their contraption of steel as though it had been a child's flimsy toy. But the Quebec disaster caused no such theological flutter. The failure of engineering was redeemed through better engineering; and the new bridge stood.

This autonomy of the human mind is an accepted fact. We feel no religious awe when casting a simple sum; the situation remains the same when the terms of the problem grow more complex; it is not altered when we reach the intricacies even of celestial mechanics. In the domain of forces which can be translated into figures, forces and figures hold sway. Laplace was voicing common sense, and Napoleon grandiloquent nonsense, in their famous dialogue: "Where is God in your system?" — "Sire, I had no need for that hypothesis."

We may well go further, and admit that this knowledge of ours is indefinitely extensible. I am willing to indulge in the wildest flights of "science fiction," that modern version of the Gothick tale. If our telescopes detect a star millions of light-

years away, that is merely an enormous extension of ancient
Chaldean lore; but it is possible for the intellect to take bolder
steps, and conceive of realms which it is as yet unable to explore.
There may dwell, in the same space and time as ours, creatures
endowed with a totally different set of senses, so that their lives
and ours, perhaps strangely similar, have no meeting point. We
can accept the possibility of other beings, perhaps with exactly
our set and range of senses, hidden from our ken in other di-
mensions of space or time. Our whole universe may be an atom
within the blood cell of some macrozoon, and so *ad infinitum*:
Pascal played earnestly with the thought of man poised between
two infinites. All this, fantastic though it may seem, does not
strain credibility any more than X-rays, radio waves and nuclear
fission. If my room is filled with inaudible and invisible programs (in all likelihood recommending some brand of soap),
may there not be other programs, fully as good, for which we
possess no receiving set?

We may go further still, and anticipate that between such interpenetrating but distinct universes some mode of communication may some day be established. Some cybernetic monster may
be devised, some radar of the unexplored, some reductor or trans-
former of energies as yet undreamt of, that will translate the nth
dimension or the nth sense into terms we can understand. Jules
Verne, H. G. Wells, Franz Werfel [1] did not actually venture
into the supernatural and the miraculous: only into the *conceivable unknown*. Their anticipations, not firmly linked with
actual knowledge, may be vain: but other anticipations, of the
same order, might be able to stand an experimental test. The
point is that the weirdest scientific utopias do not challenge the
two fundamental assumptions of rationalism: that there is a
consistent reality filling the universe, and that this reality is
ruled by immutable laws.

This is the conviction that Taine, the master against whom
I wrestled so hard in my youth, expressed in terms of religious
fervor: "Science is infallible: I know of no joy that compares

---

[1] In *Star of the Unborn*, a massive fantasy which deserved greater at-
tention than it received.

with those which come from absolute, universal, indubitable truth." [2] Here no doubt Taine put his trust not merely in the scientific spirit and the scientific method, but in the body of science, the mass of results already achieved. The "truth" which fills him with such holy enthusiasm is either a fact established for all time, or a law which can no longer be challenged: a truth static because eternal. No religion could be more dogmatic than such "positivism." It was not "science," but "scientificism," a sect which enjoyed great popularity in the materialistic generation between 1850 and 1890. Clemenceau lived and died in that simple faith; and we are told that it is the official creed of the Soviet Union. But science is not responsible for the superstitions that cling to its garments. Beyond the narrow materialism of Taine — the bitter fruit of "race, environment, and time" — we can feel the magnificent assurance of Rabelais and Descartes: the human mind conquering the material world, and even death. Much of human power, much of human dignity, would be lost if that faith should be found vain.

Now we must venture beyond the indefinitely expanding realm of Taine's science. There are realities which human reason cannot embrace. Herbert Spencer, who gave currency to the term *unknowable*, and Thomas Huxley, who was chiefly responsible for the vogue of *agnostic*, may themselves have been *scientificists* of the same brand as Taine. But whoever coined the two words, the ideas they convey are ancient and universal. The *locus* for agnosticism, recognizing the unknowable as the starkest of realities, is not Spencer's *First Principles*, but the Book of Job: "Therefore have I uttered that I understood not; things too wonderful for me, that I knew not." The sacred books are filled with the awe-inspiring thought that the ways of God are inscrutable to man, that His wisdom and His power, like His peace, pass our understanding. According to St. Thomas Aquinas, the natural law is that part of the mind of God that can be reached by human reason: the world of Spencer, Taine, and Descartes. Revelation is that part of the mind of God that

---

[2] André Chevrillon: *Taine: Formation de sa Pensée*, pp. 61–62. Many similar passages in his letters to Prévost-Paradol.

man could not reach by his own efforts, but which he is able to receive: the field of St. Thomas himself. But beyond this lies that part of the mind of God which is wholly inaccessible to man. It has never been suggested that the secret of the universe had been fully revealed to us: else we should be gods. All religions are based upon the notion of the *sacred*, that is to say of impenetrable mystery. Upon that threshhold, reason wins its ultimate victory, which is to abdicate, and yield its power to agnosticism.

There are therefore three degrees in the scale of knowledge, sacred or profane. First the *known*, attained through human reason or historical revelation. Then the *unknown-knowable*, constantly receding before expanding science and continuing revelation. And finally the *unknowable*. The frontiers between them are elastic. But if the cosmos is boundless, and man's intelligence limited, then the known will always be infinitesimal compared with the unknown (we are "gathering pebbles by the seashore"); and the knowable unknown infinitesimal compared with the unknowable.

What are the relations between these spheres? The unknowable annihilates thought and speech. Even if we grant that there is a divine spark in man, so that his mind is capable of receiving the full revelation of God, the culmination of that process would be the destruction of man himself: he would cease to be, absorbed in the whole-embracing principle. This consummation may require aeons, or it may come in a flash. In either case — the progressive deification of mankind or a sudden glimpse of the absolute — all we are and all we know would be destroyed, volatilized in the flame of the universal Presence. To grasp the unknowable is to attain nirvana.

The advance of the known into the unknown, on the contrary, is the very essence of human thought. Life is the battle line: a "truth" no longer fought over is a dead truth, part of the inorganic world. And that which saves thought from such a death is the critical spirit.

It is no paradox to claim that this holds true even of the knowledge attained through religious revelation. *The letter killeth*: beyond the letter, the spirit of man must keep up its search. Throughout the ages, there have been Doctors of the Law; but there have been prophets and mystics too, disturbers of the deadly peace. Truth does not stand still.

How are we to receive that mystic knowledge, whether imparted to a few, or found, however dimly, in every human heart? [3] The *orthodox* answer is: through the critical spirit. Again, *prove all things*. The most ardent believers do not believe everything. If Blake, Shelley, Keats, Hugo, report their visions, no sane reader accepts them at their face value. Those who most insist on the virtue of faith are most critical of every faith not their own. The purest Fundamentalist becomes a perfect Voltairian when he encounters the myths of Brahmanism, the miracles of Mohammed, the revelations of Swedenborg, the claims of the *Book of Mormon*. That critical spirit prevails even within the strictest Judeo-Christian tradition. We shall see that books claiming inspiration, and once accepted as Holy Writ, were, after severe scrutiny, relegated to the twilight zone of the Apocrypha; others were cast into outer darkness: the Book of Enoch, so influential with the early Christians, disappeared altogether for many centuries.

The Catholic Church reserves to herself the right of passing, after the most searching examination, upon the visions and the miracles which adventurous souls allege or believe to have experienced. Nothing could be more scientific in spirit and method than the role of the *Advocatus Diaboli*, who systematically doubts and requires proof, so that the truth may shine forth in perfect purity, every blemish removed. Science and scholarship are simply such advocates. They are assayers, not destroyers. If the acid test be used, only the dross will suffer.

Armand Pierhal, a very earnest and very able apologist, urges [4] the use of positive faith, silencing doubt, as a scientific instrument. A truth accepted on faith, he claims, is a working hypothesis. The believer is merely using the method, so familiar

---

[3] The subject will be discussed more fully in the third part of this book, "Faith."

[4] In *The Living God*, New York, 1950.

in geometry, of "supposing the problem solved." But in science this bold step only precedes, and does not preclude, critical examination. The hypothesis must stand repeated and various tests: else it would be rejected as "not working" or "idle." Paratroopers who cannot establish contact with the main body of the army are doomed; in the same way, the solution which we provisionally take for granted must be carefully linked back with the established facts, or be abandoned.

To claim that faith itself is a prime condition of the experiment, that certain truths refuse to manifest themselves in the material and rational world, particularly in the laboratory and the study, would simply open the flood gates of superstition. Every victim of hallucinations, every founder of a fantastic sect, can claim exemption from critical control: so long as you believe in the Ballards, the Ballard religion is unquestionably true. There was a wooden saint in some Breton church who, on the day of his festival, made a gesture of benediction over the assembly of the faithful. But they were enjoined to show their reverence by keeping their heads bowed and their eyes closed. If they did not, the saint, offended at their lack of faith, declined to perform the miracle.

It is my conviction that no "truth" which refuses the critical test can be considered as *knowable*. The test, again and again, need not, must not, be crude. There are innumerable cases in which plain logic or mechanical measurements will not prove decisive. This creates a debatable border, in which surmises and presumptions have some degree of validity. And it must be remembered also that no test is absolutely final. Pasteur proved that certain experiments concerning spontaneous generation were not valid; he could not prove that the case was closed for ever. But the general rule is *reasonably* safe: knowing and testing are one.

This does not imply the great heresy, found at the bottom of most philosophies, that "the real and the rational are one." [5]

[5] I am not advancing the argument that the rational process may err, if it works faultlessly on wrong factual premises; for to accept wrong premises is the result of some previous fault in the reasoning process.

It does not even imply that, in the boundless night of the unknown, the rational offers a compact island of light. We spoke a while ago of "the battle line": but that ever shifting line cannot be neatly marked by colored pins on the map. As in certain stages of World War II, there is no fixed front. There may be centers of resistance — stragglers, guerrillas, "hedgehogs," fortresses, "pockets," left in the rear of a victorious army: the Maginot Line was never captured, the Germans clung for weeks to the rubble of Stalingrad, and for months to a few coastal areas in France. There may be infiltrations preceding a massive attack; there may be raiders, commandos, paratroopers, jumping ahead of the general advance. Medicine, for all its marvelous progress, must acknowledge such points of stubborn resistance: we are still baffled, not only by poliomyelitis and cancer, but by the common cold. Meteorology is a "science" which still loses many skirmishes. For military operations like D-Day, or for the planning of an extensive tour by aeroplane, long-range accurate forecasting of the weather would be invaluable; and it is not forthcoming. On the other hand, astronomy is immensely ahead of most other scientific quests, and of any practical application. We can predict an eclipse, establish the existence of a planet before it is confirmed by the telescope, measure the appalling distances of the stars, while storms, earthquakes, epidemic diseases, still catch us with the briefest warning.

There is little doubt, however, that these unknown areas are knowable, although the time of their ultimate reduction cannot be predicted. We must inquire further. Are there not arrays of facts which stubbornly resist rational knowledge, not because of our present ignorance, but because of their very nature? Yet they cannot be relegated, like metaphysical problems, to the unknowable. They are with us, part of our experience, posing problems that we have to meet on the practical plane. This is the enigma of the "Dark Forces," infra-rational some of them — primitive urges, instincts, ancestral fears; some supra-rational and "dark with excess of light." No moral meaning is here attached to the word *dark*: the forces from below may be beneficent or harmful. And so may the supra-rational forces, if we admit with most religions that there are spirits of evil as well as messengers of the supreme good.

These nonrational forces must be acknowledged; and their power is such that at any moment they are capable of blasting the puny edifice of our rational world. But if they are blind (humanly speaking), there is no reason why man should follow them blindly. Here again, the critical spirit, the effort to understand, is salvation. In the present wave of romantic irrationalism — the third or fourth in the last two centuries — this doctrine may seem antiquated and shallow. So I shall borrow my illustrations from sciences which are not fossils of the classical world, but still in their lusty youth, anthropology and psychology; and from the enormous store of experience accumulated by the Christian churches.

Anthropology studies *cultures*, ways of life, complexes of beliefs, customs and institutions. Among these elements, the most distinctive is the taboo. For a member of the tribe, the taboo is a "dark force," a "thou-shalt-not" beyond reason. For the anthropologist, a taboo is a subject of study. Through comparative methods, it falls within a framework. No anthropologist is converted to the taboo he is examining. If he comes to the conclusion that the custom under consideration is beneficial, he accepts it as a sociological law, perhaps as "the wisdom of prejudice," not as a taboo, that is to say a command beyond dispute. If an anthropologist should look homeward, he would uncover, and thus dispel, taboos of his own. Anthropology performs an admirable service when it warns us: "Do not ruin the whole structure of a society under the plea of destroying superstitions: the roots are deep, and the process is delicate. Above all, do not imagine that our own set of taboos is a panacea." But caution is not blind acceptance. By studying taboos, we place ourselves beyond taboos, ours as well as those of the Trobrianders. *The darkness fades away.*

Psychoanalysts did not invent the unconscious and the subconscious, familiar to the romantics, and even to classical literature. Some psychoanalysts did invent a vocabulary, i.e., a mythology, which created both light and darkness. But the great merit of the new science is that it did not simply acknowledge the presence of the dark forces: it studied them, *in the light* of the scientific spirit. It brought the unconscious and the subconscious into the field of consciousness of the observer and of the subject. The method of approach became a therapy. The patient suffers from enslavement to the unconscious; the truth is ascertained, in its bewildering complexity; and it is the truth that brings healing, which is freedom. Anthropology and psychoanalysis are not gospels of submission, but of enlightenment. Know thyself, know thy society, know thy mind, and thou shalt be whole.

The Christian church, to use the most familiar simile, is an army arrayed against the Prince of Darkness. Some believe that mere defiance will suffice: Satan exists, and I refuse to serve him. But as a rule it is recognized that the Tempter is too insidious, too plausible, to be chased away by an inkpot hurled at his head. To guard against his snares, we need, not merely a sudden illumination, but a steady light, and a constant effort. All great believers search their consciences. The Catholic Church, through auricular confession and the careful training of directors, has provided for centuries the most elaborate of psychoanalytical clinics. The solution is certainly not to jump shuddering into the abyss. We must face the facts of temptation, and establish connections between these facts. Liberty, love, power, conceal possibilities of evil, yet they cannot be dismissed offhand. Resignation itself may be either a virtue or a trap. *Conduct* means steering, not drifting.

I shall affirm a little later in this "Discourse," and particularly in the third part of this book, that I have faith in faith. We must acknowledge the supra-rational as an urge and a guidance which reason cannot provide, just as we must acknowledge the infrarational, the crazy, the brutish, as a very real obstacle and a relentless foe. But, even in the murk of German Romanticism, no sane man will unresistingly obey the impulse to rape and to kill; none will accept without examination every hunch that flits darkly across his mind; none will admit as sober fact every lurid vision, a stranger's or even his own. When reason is silent, the strange voice within may be that of the beast, the fiend, or the angel. This voice did not originate in reason; but reason preserves the right and the duty to examine the voice's credentials. Not by the yardstick of formal logic, not by the loose statistics of material facts: but by a scrupulous and orderly inquiry.

Awareness, clear-eyed and stout-hearted, combating chaos: such is the goal, not of science merely, from mathematics to psychology, but of morality and religion as well. Granted that reason is only the testing instrument, not the motive power: the test remains indispensable. No doubt there comes a moment when we must let ourselves go, in love, in poetic inspiration, in mystic communion. But we must be sure that the light that leads us is not darkness. Impulses are neither to be crushed as irrational, nor blindly followed as deeper than all reason. Let us never lose sight of the Apostle's great words: "Prove all things." He serves best, loves best, believes best, who best understands.

Rabelais's noble phrase, "Science without conscience is the ruin of the soul," is constantly quoted without becoming trite. But we should remember that in French *conscience* means three things which ought to be inseparable: conscientiousness, consciousness, conscience. To mean well is not enough: you must also know exactly what you mean. Conscience, ardent, unenlightened, undisciplined, or narrowed and warped by a blind dogma, is actually the greatest power for evil in human history. The brutalities of primitives, morons, or perverts have killed their thousands; but unreflecting conscience has slain its millions. Fanaticism is "conscience without science." Hitler's conscience was clear: he acted to promote an ideal which to him was sacred and beyond dispute. When Napoleon murdered the Duke of Enghien with the merest parody of judicial forms, Boullay de la Meurthe (it ought to have been Fouché or Talleyrand) commented: "It is worse than a crime: it is a blunder." There is deep moral meaning in that cynical remark. The range of crime is short, but an error may be the source of incalculable evils. Wars increase in horror as they grow more "conscientious," i.e., more ideological. A fight for dynastic prestige, or even for a province, could be half-hearted, and be kept, as in the eighteenth century, within the rules of a gentlemanly game. The battle over, the contestants shook hands and arranged for a marriage between their families. A fight for principles, and above all for religious convictions, soaring above interests and reason, unleashes the Fiend.

The remedy is not to shrug all principles away, but to examine them critically, i.e., scrupulously, *conscientiously,* in the light of facts and orderly thinking. When the elements of the problem have been brought to full *consciousness,* then let *conscience* be the judge. I feel confident that the path chosen by enlightened conscience will be that not of brutality, but of reasonableness.

In this plea for consciousness, or intelligence, I may seem to be emphasizing unduly the quest for "scientific" truth. I repeat that I escaped over half a century ago from the thrall of Taine. I do not believe that "the truth," if it be of a scientific nature, will suffice to make us free. It is possible for factual knowledge to be true, yet totally irrelevant to human purposes. A fact does not become science until it is brought into relation with other facts. The connections thus established — ideas, methods, hypotheses, laws — are the substance of scientific truth. But so far as human conduct is concerned, the result is neutral. There are truths which are morally indifferent: from the number of the stars to the matrimonial customs of *Mantis religiosa.* There are ugly and obnoxious truths: poisons have their place in reality. The consistent realist takes things as they are: if the water from a river brings disease, it brings disease, and that is all there is to it. The *pure* scientist (not a philanthropist in disguise) holds the balance even: "Well done, bacteria! Well done, antiseptic!" When, in the positivistic era, pure science claimed leadership in human thought and action, Brunetière was justified in announcing its bankruptcy. Science is necessary to focus facts and thoughts in our consciousness; but it is not for science to decide.

Decision is an act of the will. Here we are brought back to Descartes. And we have to meet another formidable phantom:

the problem of freedom. Like solipsism, determinism (and its equivalents on the philosophical and theological planes, fatalism, predestination, Providence) cannot be disproved by logic. The world *must* be a concatenation of causes and effects: an endless concatenation, not originating miraculously in a causeless First Cause. There again, we may leave the metaphysicians to fight it out in the impalpable. On earth, we live and move as though we had at least the illusion of a choice; and a persistent, consistent illusion is a good pragmatic definition for a reality.

It is obvious to the common man that he is ruled by inexorable law: he falls, he hungers, he sleeps, he dies. The absolute believer denies such subjection: faith conquers gravity and death. Still, when it comes to moving mountains, Christian contractors put their faith in bulldozers. Within this vast mesh of cosmic forces, man has a degree of apparent autonomy. He is not ruled by statistical law: he is not bound to die at threescore and ten. He cannot escape hunger: but he can eat what he pleases at the time he chooses. He is the prey of blind Eros: but he need not be the median in Dr. Kinsey's Report. He can pick out his mate, or even repress the urge altogether. Necessity being taken for granted, the field of human endeavor is that of freedom. Of course it is infinitesimal from the point of view of the absolute. But it is our world. It means much to us. Perhaps everything.

It is strange that the greatest exponents of Necessity, philosophical, religious or scientific, should also have been the greatest exemplars of will power. None is so *determined* as the man who believes in determinism. The fatalism of Islam resulted in a tremendous surge of energy. There was no flabby "quietism" about the Calvinists and the Jansenists. Napoleon believed in Fate, in his star, and in the Force of Things: but he acted as though he believed in himself. The materialistic determinism of Marx led to the triumph of the heroic will, in Marx himself and in the founders of the Soviet Union.[6]

[6] According to Raymond Bauer (*The New Man in Soviet Psychology*, Harvard University Press, 1952), the Party line has shifted from sheer

But the will is not the ultimate: we will because we desire; and desire, even though served by the most relentless will, is futile if we ignore hard facts. Any man can prove to himself that he is free, that he can perform a "gratuitous act," by hurling himself from the top story of the Empire State Building: but he will not live to gloat over his triumph. It was argued that "the will of the people" had the right to choose collective slavery as a demonstration of freedom: but it was a will that despaired of itself. The will to destroy, the will to hurt, is a weakness, not a virtue. Medea, whose splendid self-assertion we quoted above, killed her children to spite their father: but it was in impotent rage, because she could not bend her husband to her will. Heaven save us from *will-full* men!

It is not sufficient for the will to be "enlightened," in the sense of "well informed." Hitler knew clearly whom he wanted to kill, and how to kill them by the most efficient means: neither awareness nor intensity was lacking in his case. It is the direction that matters. What is needed is *good* will. Not in the sense of easy-going friendly acquiescence: such good will is no will at all. But in the strenuous meaning of energy bent toward a worthy goal. In a word, above the instincts, the intelligence, the will of men, there must be a *sense*, the magnetic pole of our efforts. I shall not attempt at this stage to define "the good." I can only voice my conviction that it can be reached neither by the dark forces unenlightened, nor by intelligence undirected, nor by self-will blinded by its own power. My effort so far has been to defend reason, not as a substitute for faith, but as the indispensable servant of faith. In other terms, I am seeking, not to destroy, but to purify, the conception of faith.

---

determinism to a new insistence on the creative will. The results of this New Freedom have not yet become apparent.

CHAPTER V

The enlightenment

$\mathcal{I}$ am no worshipper of the past, neither of the eighteenth century, nor of the sixteenth, nor of the thirteenth, nor of the first. With a very different ring, the voice of Molière: "The ancients are the ancients, and we are the people of to-day," echoes that of Jesus: "Let the dead bury their dead."

If this were not my *Bottle in the Sea*, written solely for the satisfaction of my own conscience, the present section would undoubtedly have been omitted. I am shifting for a time from the philosophical plane to the historical: I am aware that this will not deepen the inquiry or strengthen the argument. On the contrary, I am deliberately weakening my case by linking it with the *Philosophes* of the Age of Reason, fossils whose unhonored bones are buried deep under the alluvions of two hundred years.

I am not moved by an ingrained prejudice in their favor: I was not brought up in the reverence of the Philosophes. Indeed I had to fight my way back to them, against some of my most respected masters. Least of all am I seeking historical warrant for my convictions.

The plain fact is that I recognize the kinship between my own thought and that of Locke, Montesquieu, Voltaire, Hume, Gibbon, just as close friends of mine feel themselves in deep harmony with Luther, Calvin, St. Augustine, and St. Paul. The quest of awareness which I am urging is ancient: it is the "Know thyself" of Greek philosophy. But in history, it has a definite name, *les Lumières, die Aufklärung,* the Enlightenment.

The Ahriman of that Ormuzd is the cult of darkness, or

Obscurantism. This antagonism does not neatly coincide with any sharp division between schools, parties or creeds. No doubt there is a reactionary obscurantism with Hamann, the Magian of the North, and with Joseph de Maistre; but there is a revolutionary obscurantism with Rousseau and with Blake. There is an obscurantist strain among the classicists. It is unmistakable in the purest of them all, Racine, whose characters are hurled by dark passions into madness and death. And there is a striving toward the light in a most undeniable romanticist like Shelley. The obscurantist element has been strong throughout the ages among Christian thinkers: in modern times, we find it in Kierkegaard *redivivus*, in Léon Bloy, in Unamuno, in Reinhold Niebuhr. But orthodoxy, under the banner of St. Thomas Aquinas, stands for sweetness and light: revelation and reason in close harmony compel darkness to recede. The two contending forces coexist in the same men: Goethe sought to create mystery and awe in his darkling myth of the Mothers; and his dying lips demanded: "More light!" Hugo, on the intellectual surface, was an apostle of light, a heavier, more eloquent Voltaire; in the depths, he was Tennyson's "weird Titan, cloud-weaver of phantasmal hopes and fears."

The conflict is timeless. Yet history is not a delusion. The past is still obscurely with us. The fact that the Philosophes were derided by the Romanticists, and swept contemptuously aside by the Realists, is influencing our subconscious mind today. We dare not freely follow our thought, when it seems to be leading us back to the antiquated frivolities of the Pompadour era. We treat Voltaire with Voltairian irony: perhaps it serves him right. His grin still haunts us, but as a warning, not as a guide. I have no desire to be led by the ghost of Voltaire; but I want even less to be hampered by the ghost of anti-Voltairianism. If I happen to agree with the Patriarch, I shall be a most willing fellow traveler: he is pleasanter company than Karl Marx or Herbert Spencer.

The obscurantists, true to their spirit and method, have created a thick cloud which veils the Enlightenment from us. Some of their assertions are easy to disprove: far less easy to dispel, for the black legend they embody influences good scholars even today. Others are far more subtle, although in my opinion no less specious. Others still contain a strong element of factual truth.

To begin with, the Enlightenment was not ruled by crude formal logic. Not only did it inherit the "reasonableness" of the seventeenth century, but its acknowledged master, the guide of Montesquieu, Voltaire, d'Alembert, was Bacon and not Descartes. These men believed, not in abstract constructions, but in critical thought, serious inquiry, experimental science. This, incidentally, disposes of the accusation that they were frivolous. They smiled the delightful smile so well caught by La Tour, but they were also hard workers. Bayle's *Historical Dictionary*, Montesquieu's *Spirit of Laws*, Voltaire's *Century of Louis XIV* and *Essay on Manners*, Diderot's mighty *Encyclopaedia*, Buffon's monumental *Natural History*, Gibbon's *Decline and Fall*, are massive achievements, hard to match in any period. This very list disposes of a third charge: that the Philosophes lacked historical sense. They did not worship the past, like some Romanticists, for its picturesque or sentimental appeal. They refused to accept without examination "the wisdom of prejudice." But it was their enemy Rousseau who grandly asserted: "First of all, let us brush aside all the facts!" The Philosophes studied the past earnestly, diligently. Montesquieu and Voltaire were the founders of modern history, emerging at last from the welter of chronicles, breaking the inflexible framework of dogma. Gibbon is still read not merely with delight, but with profit. It is frivolous antiquarianism, the Wardour Street or Ye Olde Shoppe school, that is hopelessly out of date now.

Nothing is more shallow than the accusation that the Enlightenment ignored the Dark Forces. These men believed firmly in the devil lurking in every heart: Voltaire called him *l'Infâme* and devoted the most active part of his career to wrestling with his power. *L'Infâme* appears in the brute, the degenerate, the beast in human form. But he is infinitely more potent in the shape of perverse self-righteousness. Then, under the cloak of superstition and even of dogmatism, he sums up and intensifies the brutal impulses which lead men to fiendish ferocity. *L'Infâme* loomed, an obscene idol, over Buchenwald, Ausschwitz, and Katyn Forest. It coined the name "Operation Killer." *L'Infâme* dwells in the hearts of infidels and atheists, but also in those of believers, heretics and orthodox alike. For honest error, the Philosophes had nothing but amused tolerance. They were even ready to dally with pleasant fable:

Ah! Croyez-moi: l'erreur a son mérite.

But the urge to enslave, to torture, and to kill could not be encountered with urbane irony. It had to be fought in life-and-death battle, even though it wore, sacrilegiously, a sacred mask. No flippancy, no inane smirking, in such a combat. If the Philosophes smiled, their smile was a weapon; at times, it was the shining forth of their legitimate joy in arduous work faithfully done.

When the Philosophes were so clearly aware of the Dark Forces in the world and in man's heart, they cannot with any fairness be accused of bleating optimism. It was not they, but Leibniz, who contended that "all was for the best in the best possible world." In the face of a great natural catastrophe, the Lisbon earthquake, Voltaire felt poignantly that this world was not run according to the rules of human reason. He saw with horror the Absurd lurking behind the smiling face of Nature. It was Rousseau, most ardent of the Obscurantists, who challenged Voltaire's tragic view of the cosmos. And Voltaire replied with *Candide*, which no sane reader would consider a breviary of optimism like *Pippa Passes*. Those men knew that evil — human evil, social evil, cosmic evil — was no delusion. But they refused to bow before the Dark Forces of Unreason. If these forces crush us, we can still, with Pascal, rise superior to their brutal might; and before they crush us, we can clear a small plot where reasoned care will prevail. We can cultivate our garden.

Let us till our little plot: only in such a modest, cautious manner did the Enlightenment believe in *progress*. Yet the word clings to them as a term of reproach: whoever holds that things need not steadily go from bad to worse must be a fool. There again we must carefully eschew the metaphysical. From the point of view of eternity, the idea of progress is utter foolishness: but so is motion, and life itself, for the Absolute kills human thought altogether. On the plane of our experience, we act as though progress were desirable and possible. Those who sneer at the Enlightenment do so because, in their own conceit, they have *progressed* beyond the shallowness of that benighted time. We take it for granted that we can improve the health of mankind. Psychology does not merely describe, but seeks to alleviate and even cure mental ailments. All education is based on some faith in progress: we assume that men can learn to live wholesomer lives. All legislation *claims* to be "progressive": i.e., it is meant to check certain evils and promote the good of the community: certainly Messrs. Taft and Hartley had no desire to make economic and social conditions worse. Reinhold Niebuhr and Clarence Macartney, when they teach and preach, are apostles of progress: they are home missionaries, they strive to expand the domain of the truth as they understand it, in the hope that the truth will make us increasingly free. Even though all human history were but a dubious battle against decadence, progress would at any rate retard our doom. It is a tempting thought that, as in *Through the Looking Glass,* we have to run faster and faster, in order barely to hold our own.

The common prejudice against progress — a prejudice supported by men of very great distinction — is due, I believe, to three misapprehensions, innocent or willful. The first is the defense of vested interests. Any change, demanded in the name of progress, is a challenge to the *beati possidentes,* be their possession some material property, a privileged position, a skill, an orthodoxy: any acquisition or achievement that can be turned into a citadel. In resisting change, these men are honestly upholding the good life, i.e., the one they enjoy. There is hardly any progress that does not spell decay for some legitimate business, craft, status, or ideology. You cannot give full civil rights to men of a darker breed without threatening white supremacy.

You cannot increase the responsibilities of labor in the management of an enterprise without whittling down the ancient right of the "masters" to do as they please with their own. If we did "progress" in the path of Christianity, that is to say of gentleness and brotherly love, lawyers and soldiers would be out of a job. To discredit the very idea of progress is a masterly move in the upholding of the status quo: it provides a background of distrust against any particular proposal. Reformers are by definition progressists, even when they advocate, as I frequently do, a return to paths long forsaken; and the Thrones and Dominations do not welcome reform.

A second specious plea is to identify the idea of progress with its caricatures: automatic progress and material progress. Change is incessant, but at various rates and in various directions. It inevitably involves decay as well as growth: if we were bacteria instead of men, we would consider an epidemic as a boom, a medical counter-offensive as a disaster. Even from the purely human point of view, how uncertain, how precarious has been the road! In art, in philosophy, in religion, perhaps even in government, there are lost heights which have not yet been recovered. We are astounded to find, in the middle ages, by the side of the crassest superstition and the noblest flight of mysticism, certain strangely modern appeals to free thought, humanity, political liberty, social justice: appeals which would ring clear and bold in our days. Yet heretics and rebels were crushed, not merely by brute force, but under the whole weight of the law and of official learning. In the sixteenth century, the oppressed peasants may have been right against the princes and Martin Luther, and Servetus against Calvin: but they perished. The weary path of human progress is lined with Calvaries. But this tragic record does not absolve us from our plain duty: whenever we see suffering, we should seek some means of alleviation. In purpose, at any rate, progress and healing are one.

The question of material progress is tangled. It is easy enough to smile at the complacency of Voltaire in *Le Mondain*, or at the Rotarian strains of Alfred Lord Tennyson:

Fifty years of ever-broadening Commerce!
Fifty years of ever-brightening Science!
Fifty years of ever-widening Empire!

Statistics of automobiles, cinemas, television sets, plumbing fixtures, and even of universities and hospitals, are impressive, and well-nigh meaningless. Rather a Mahatma Gandhi in his loin cloth than a prince of racketeers in the glory of his Florida estate. The men whom we most revere in the past enjoyed none of our gadgets. When I was a schoolboy, many of our proudest achievements were awkward infants; some, like aviation, were still dreams; others, like radar and nuclear fission, were undreamt of even by a Jules Verne. Yet I knew men who, in wisdom, good will, courtesy, would still be an honor to the human race. When a stockbroker, supreme flower and perfect symbol of our civilization, wants to rise to his full height, he goes roughing it in the Northern wilds. All this is trite enough, and would not even be mentioned, but for the fact that in the great international debate, we are still urging our material wealth and power as a decisive *moral* argument. We are all Little Jack Horners: see what plums we have pulled, and what good little boys we must be!

There is, however, a serious as well as a vulgar side to this problem. Progress in the sciences, pure and applied, is undeniable. Aristotle may have had a better scientific mind than even Einstein: but Aristotle's learning has been left a long way behind. This progress, accelerating at an appalling rate, has not been brought into harmony with our moral progress; and if our hearts be evil, science can multiply the dire effects a thousandfold. But what is the remedy? Certainly not to curb science with "the wisdom of prejudice." It would cripple science without liberating us. Is there nothing we can learn from the scientific spirit, which is winning such unbelievable victories? Not materialism: that simply defines the field of science; but a method, at the same time cautious and bold, and above all scrupulously honest; a method which rejects equally conceit, compromise, and make-believe. It should not be impossible to cultivate the same virtues in the service of the good as the scientists bring to

the service of the true. But the first step would be to acknowledge the good — still to be defined — as a desirable end; and
the second would be to explore the human implications of the
good as fearlessly, as cautiously, as conscientiously as the scientists investigate their own domain. Give us seekers for the good
equipped with the critical spirit and the experimental method:
then we shall have men to match our cyclotrons.

The last objection to the progressivism of the Enlightenment
is a factual one. The Philosophes were poor prophets. They did
not foresee the formidable opposition, and the still more formidable deviations, which were to shatter their dream. They were
hopelessly mistaken in their time-table: even as were the early
Christians, who believed that the kingdom of God was literally
at hand. Neither did we, thirty years ago, anticipate the rise
of a Hitler or a Stalin: which does not prove that our hope for
a liberal world was altogether vain.

This is but the brutal argument of Brennus: *Vae victis!* The
Enlightenment failed, as romantic humanitarianism was to fail
in 1848, as the realism of the Bismarckian era failed two generations ago: what is history but a record of shipwrecks? The
age of urbane reason was followed by a prolonged rebarbariza-
tion of the world; the total wars inaugurated in self-defense by
the French Revolution are still darkening our lives. There was
a generation which stridently claimed to be "lost"; the fourteenth
and fifteenth centuries have been called, not without reason,
"lost centuries," at any rate north of the Alps. In the same
way, the long period from the rise of Romanticism to our own
days might be called a long wandering in the Waste Land, an
age of the lost. No intimation of the dawn: fears and doubts,
children of the night, are still increasing.

But the Enlightenment cannot be blamed for the criminal
follies of its foes. The Philosophes were not the instigators of the
Terror, but its victims. Condorcet was harried to death, affirm-
ing to the last his faith in the perfectibility of the human mind.
Lavoisier the scientist, André Chénier the poet, Anacharsis
Clootz "the friend of the human race," the more equivocal
Chaumette, who had staged a harmless pageant in honor of

Reason, were sent to the scaffold. Thomas Paine, Lafayette, Lakanal — the author of a noble plan for national education — were driven into exile. Yes, the Revolution became the prey of the Dark Powers, and it was one of the deepest tragedies in the annals of the world. But it was not because the Enlightenment assumed control: it was because it was swept aside. The contest was (and is still today) waged between barbarians. Those whom Matthew Arnold so aptly called by that name, the Barbarians from above, the feudal aristocracy, unwilling to give up their privileges and their superstitions, first attempted to stem the Revolution by the force of bayonets. Then arose the barbarians from below, the primitives, called to arms in the name of Rousseau to meet the threat of reaction. So Reason and Liberty were attacked, and defended, by naked force. It was force, not principles, that triumphed with Napoleon; it was force, not liberty or reason, that won the final victory over Napoleon.[1]

Had England and America whole-heartedly supported the French Revolution in 1793, the victory of liberty and peace would have been hastened by decades. A *might-have-been*: but unless history admits that "whatever is, is right" — including Tamerlane, Hitler and Stalin — it is constantly weighing *might-have-beens*. We blame Russia today for being Malenkov's, when she *might have been* Kerensky's or Tsar Michael's.

The Enlightenment may be a lost cause: it is not a bad cause. And two centuries are but a flash even in the brief record of civilized men. The pure Christianity of the Waldensians suffered defeat; but Protestantism was its vindication. Between the *Scientia Experimentalis* of Friar Roger Bacon and the *Novum Organum* of Sir Francis Bacon, there were interminable generations. Hope deferred is not proved false.

The great indictment against the Philosophes is not that they desired progress, but that they miscalculated its possible rate.

[1] It must be noted that the Enlightenment did not fail altogether in America: Franklin, Washington, Jefferson were not repudiated. It was not until our own days that we resolutely turned against the rule of Reason, by expunging from our Constitution the First Amendment, which contains the essence of a liberal polity.

They were accused of failing to gauge the geological slowness
of human evolution. Mankind, it was said, proceeds not by
deliberate thought and determined action, but by imperceptible
unconscious growth. Such was the thesis of Edmund Burke,
repeated by all conservatives to the present day.

The case is not so simple as it appeared to Burke's powerful
but narrowly dogmatic mind. Even in physical nature, there
are leaps and bounds: mutations in the realm of heredity, catastrophes in the august unfolding of geological phenomena. Our
eyes have seen the birth of a volcano; and the titanic disruption
of rock strata in certain mountains can hardly be explained by
imperceptible surrection and erosion. Minute changes, obscurely continuing for ages, may culminate in a dramatic event.
The fall of the Campanile in Venice was not due to a sudden
push, yet it was instantaneous. The mighty European empires,
Austria, Russia, Germany, went with the wind a generation
ago: a few years before, they seemed unassailable. Slavery as
an institution was backed by the majesty of millennia. It had
withstood Christianity and the Age of Reason, yet it disappeared
by a stroke of the pen. You never know whether a giant has
feet of gilded clay until you try pushing him down. Who knows
but the denunciations of preachers, thinkers, and poets throughout the ages, and the curses of common men, have not hol-
lowed out the idol War, formidable as it may still appear to
timid souls? The fight against war is as ancient as war itself:
keep up a while longer the effort of centuries, and the faith in
human holocausts may be exorcized from our minds. Some diseases are long drawn out; some are brief; but death is always
instantaneous. And resurrection is an infrequent occurrence: a
dead taboo, a dead superstition, a dead regime, are very dead
indeed.

Granted the end may be sudden: but are there sudden be-
ginnings? Cautious minds find it hard to believe in conversion,
individual or collective. According to the orthodox disciples of
Burke, no man and no people in history ever turned from the
error of their ways, and, with a new hope, embraced a new
rule of life. They deny the possibility of an awakening: man-

kind slumbers on, moving sluggishly in its uneasy sleep. For awakening, like conversion, like birth, like death, is a new departure, and there never was anything new under the sun. Yet against Burke's doctrine, history records awakenings, some tragic, some throbbing with joy. Aviation was a dream for millennia, a baffling quest for generations. Then, slowly prepared, but sudden, the miracle happened: I was a full grown man when the first aeroplane rose from the ground. The unchangeable East is altering under our eyes at a rate which we cannot gauge. Once Crèvecœur hailed "the American" as a New Man, and he was not wholly wrong. There may be a new humanity struggling to be born under our very eyes. I fully accept "the inevitability of gradualness" but the fall into a chasm, the soaring of a jet plane, the course of a cannon ball, are as "gradual" as the progress of a snail: no intermediate step can be skipped. There is no scientific reason for accepting the snail's pace as the norm. It was not unreasonable then for the Philosophes to fight as though privileges, prejudices, and superstitions would yield to their onslaught. The confidence indispensable to action implies a degree of wishful thinking: if we want to win, we must first hope to win.

As a matter of fact, it was not the millennial hopes of the Enlightenment that proved its undoing, but on the contrary its realistic modesty. The Philosophes proposed reforms, sweeping and accelerating reforms no doubt, but reforms still, not challenging the continuous development of civilization. They felt themselves the heirs of the Renaissance, and of Bacon, and of the apostles of reason in the classical age. They did not promise a new heaven and a new earth: read Voltaire's *Vision of Babouc*. They sought to build a better road: not to try an adventurous short cut, and least of all to leap in the dark. It was the religious revival, well exemplified in Wesley, that urged the possibility of salvation through a single act of faith. It was Rousseau who proposed to break away from the painfully built-up tradition of the arts and sciences. The enemies of the Enlightenment put their trust in magic: they invoke the *chthonic* forces (chthonic is a marvelous word to create awe), the blood and the soil, the wisdom of prejudice, any abracadabra that will serve as an excuse from modest thought and persistent effort.

The eclipse of the Enlightenment — for I do not admit its permanent extinction — was mainly due to three causes. The first was the use of force: Minerva should rely upon her own weapons, not on an alliance with Mars. The Revolution was to some extent the Enlightenment in armor: but the armor stifled the Revolution. It is possible for man to survive through the clash of arms; not so for ideas. Ideas are doomed under conditions which deny their validity. Even a cold war freezes thought. Both the French and the American Revolutions were compelled to take up arms in self-defense. But geographical isolation saved America: for generations, foreign wars seemed to us alien and remote. France, entirely surrounded by foes, was not so fortunate.

The second cause was the fact that the Enlightenment remained identified with the middle class: a substantial, educated bourgeoisie, with a sprinkling of liberal nobles, and, in Paris at least, a fair number of intelligent craftsmen. But that class, attacking privileges, had no thought of abandoning its own, which it considered as a just reward. The bourgeois revolution decreed death against any one who should propose an "agrarian law," [2] that is to say a socialistic or share-the-wealth measure. Moreover, that class, long associated with the monarchy, inherited the pride of the dynastic state. To the present day, bourgeois nations "draw the sword" in vindication of their "honor." So "Progress" was entrusted to the care of a class which, in two all-important questions, looked obstinately backward. That class had refrained from educating the masses to responsibility. When Danton said: "Next to bread, education is the most essential need of the people," it was already too late. An "appeal to the people" in 1792 was in fact an appeal not to reason but to the mob.[3]

---

[2] A classical allusion, in the style of the times, to the "agrarian laws" proposed by the Gracchi.
[3] I am told that, nearly two centuries later, the situation is the same

The third cause is of a cultural nature. The Enlightenment, so bold in its thinking, remained timidly pseudoclassical in art and literature. The apostles of progress were epigones: if the tales that Voltaire dashed off in a few days have retained their sparkling grace, his ambitious poems and his tragedies have at best a pale lunar sheen. Europe sought to escape from the everlasting imitation of imitations — the tyranny of "good taste" — by rushing into the primitive, the barbaric, and even the insane. Because Reason appeared in neat obsolete garments, Reason was rejected as drab and timid. The Enlightenment did not recognize openly enough the necessity for adventure, the exhilaration of the battle line into mystery. Correcting abuses is a retrospective attitude. Aristotle's profound theory of tragedy holds true in this case. The Enlightenment was a noble spirit which suffered defeat through an inner flaw. And that flaw, *reasonableness,* was but the excess of its essential virtue. The truly reasonable man must be ready to venture beyond reason. So this brilliant century died of its spiritual drabness, this generous century suffered from a bourgeois narrowness of mind and heart. The defeat was not undeserved; but it was a tragedy for mankind.

I need hardly say that this defense of the Enlightenment is not intended as an apology for the eighteenth century. The picture of French society on the eve of the Revolution popularized by *A Tale of Two Cities* is a melodramatic caricature. But I do not belong to the idyllic, or comic-opera schools of historians, like Franz Funck-Brentano, who view the whole of France under Louis XVI as a happy Trianon village. The victory of the Enlightenment was as yet very incomplete. There was no lack of squalor and ignorance below, of pride and cruelty above. Some of the squires were healthy brutes, some of the courtiers were handsome beasts of prey. The line I would follow does not lead back to Voltaire, but forward from Voltaire. What would the progress of science and industry, so characteristic of the

in Latin America, particularly in Argentina. The "enlightened" bourgeoisie had ignored the masses; and the *descamisados* rallied to Perón.

late eighteenth century, have yielded if it could have escaped the reaction, intellectual, political, and tribal, that marked the nineteenth? For a hundred and fifty years, we have been attempting to guide the formidable young giant with ideas which were growing obsolete under Louis XIV: need we wonder if he gets beyond our control?

PART II

Dream

THE IVORY TOWER

"L'art est un jeu lucide
aux confins du réel,
du rêve et de la folie."

Three idols

$\mathcal{I}$ am conscious of my personal equation: I have been a student of the humanities all my life, and my professional interests have distorted me into a "humanist." So I am tempted to offer a humanistic interpretation of human affairs, just as others view the world from the theocratic, the mechanical, the biological, or the economic standpoints. Molière has enriched French folklore with the character of Monsieur Josse, the jeweler persuaded that jewelry is the cure for all our infirmities. Josse-like, many Americans put their trust in bigger and better business, and old soldiers profess that there is no substitute for victory. "You have wares to sell: *vous êtes orfèvre, Monsieur Josse.*"

So, as a teacher of literature, I was tempted to read history in the light of my own craft, and I ascribed the failure of the Enlightenment to the limitations of pseudoclassical taste. The ardor, the generosity, the sense of adventure which made the eighteenth century a new and greater Renaissance were hemmed in and dulled by social and artistic conventions. The result was exquisite at times: but the perfection thus attained left a sense of futility. It was impossible to be more elegant than Madame de Pompadour or wittier than Voltaire: but a *nec plus ultra* is an *impasse.* No more worlds of beauty to discover and conquer: all that remained to do was to remove minor blemishes. But taste, when reduced to fastidiousness, is self-defeating. It can lead only, as Voltaire prophetically felt, to the utter weariness of the Venetian Senator, Pococurante. A man whose greatest achievement is to detect flaws sentences himself to live in a world of flaws.

A revolution in taste preceded the political revolution. Man escaped from stale perfumes into the open fields. The cult of sophistication, through a Hegelian process, created the cult of the primitive. Not "enlightened taste," but the untutored, the spontaneous, the naïve, could release "genius," kindle "enthusiasm," reach "the sublime." Delicate brows might be lifted and delicate lips curled: but the barbarians triumphed, because they brought the promise of life, fresh and eager. At least they could tear away outward forms which, embalmed in their self-satisfaction, were manifestly dead.

This was the rebellion of an art which sought close harmony with nature, within and without, against an art which had become pure artifice. This upheaval, a challenge to civilization, was a peril. What can follow the irruption of the barbarians, if not the Dark Ages? I abhor revolutions: in a violent transvaluation of all values, the delicate is invariably doomed, and the crude flourishes for a while, perhaps for a very long while. "We are nothing: let us be everything": these words that the Marxian International anthem cribbed from Abbé Siéyès always impressed me with their abysmal unwisdom. If only the Enlightenment had found it possible to welcome the new spirit whole-heartedly, in art and in religion! The miracle almost happened, in the robust and vivid personality of Diderot. Diderot had said: *"Elargissez Dieu!"*: widen the conception of God, or, more literally, set God free. He could have been instrumental in setting the human mind free, not from antiquated superstitions only, but from the conventions of enlightened taste. He might have been a more dynamic Goethe, and at the crucial moment; whereas Goethe could only soar above the strife, in Olympian impotence. But Diderot was absorbed in an enormous material task, the editing of the great *Encyclopaedia*. So the indispensable man was not available, and the Obscurantists, Rousseau, Blake, Burke, and their respective cohorts, could intone: "Deepen our darkness, we beseech Thee, O Lord!"

The result was undoubtedly a great release of artistic creativeness, particularly in the purest of the arts, music, and in the deepest, lyric poetry. It was also a great revival of religion, or perhaps of religiosity, as a conscious distinct power. If, in the chequered evolution of mankind, Rousseauism may be called another Fall, we are tempted to say again: *"Felix culpa!"* The Voltairians were all too mature: poets, believers, lovers, and even barbarians, have the poignant elusive charm of adolescence. The world of the Philosophes was an interminable afternoon; if the Romanticists invoked and created darkness, it was with a presentiment of the dawn.

As "a rationalist — within reason," I have steadily refused to deny that strange gleam on the horizon. (It is impossible to speak sympathetically of Romanticism without falling into its idiom.) Blake, Coleridge, Shelley, Keats, bring to us a tremor that Pope never knew. At least, they did not preach that "whatever is, is right," the most futile creed under the sun, and the most despairing. I still maintain that our practical life should be guided by *reason,* the proper understanding and organizing of circumstances; but we must never forget that reason is the path, not the goal. Romanticism focused for us the notion of the quest: the undefined, the unattainable for which we yearn is the ultimate reality. In this respect, the deepest forms of art and religion are one, and one also with the only love that is worthy of the name. All three are above the law: for the law is only the dead hand of the past. All three have a living law of their own: poetry, like "the heart" and like faith, has its reasons which reason cannot fathom. This deliberate spurning of mere reason was the great promise of Romanticism: it opened the road to Xanadu.

In hours of tragic confusion, common sense has the appeal of a vanished Arcadia: O to read Pope in a shady nook! Yet, I repeat, *common sense is not enough.* Let reason prevail, served by her marvelous handmaiden science, and what shall it profit us? A Bellamy Utopia is no Heavenly City. I am familiar with every nook and cranny of it: my intellect has dwelt in it ever since I was able to read. I have been for decades a citizen of that "Universal Socialist Republic" hailed by Charles Péguy. It is an attainable minimum, and our conscience will not let us rest until it is attained; but it is not an ideal. On the most hum-drum material plane, my Utopia has been a reality. My essential liberties have never (yet) been infringed upon. I have never known insecurity and want. I have been free from bodily fear: serving in two armies, active in two wars, I have known neither wound nor even discomfort. I have enjoyed tolerable health, and I am still able to do a good day's work. Indefinite longevity would help very little: I am not interested in going back to Methuselah. I want every one to be as fortunate as I have been: but I *want infinitely more.*

No doubt an intellectual Utopia promises unlimited expansion — on the material plane: not fifty years merely, but aeons of ever-broadening commerce, of ever-brightening science, of ever-widening empire. The vistas thus opened are impressive, and unspeakably dull. The enormous literature of space adventure is already stale. When we circle the moon, or even Pluto, our response will be a shrug: "Is this all?" I agree with Franz Werfel in his *Star of the Unborn*: power over nature is magnificent, but it is vanity.

What remains? One path is open: the exploration of the human mind. Not sociology, but psychology is the supreme science: Fourier saw deeper than Comte. But I can see the end. Suppose the psychologists could make all men sane, free from delusions, free from anguish: I have been sane most of my life, free at least from the most noxious forms of psychoses, *and again it is not enough.* Suppose we could be trained to a high degree of mind reading and telepathy: what then? The minds thus revealed might not be worth reading, the telepathic messages not worth receiving. I can only foresee, in a psychological Utopia, the need for an elaborate technique for protecting our privacy. Psychology, I trust, will provide weapons against psychological burglars and intruders. I can hear the harassed cry: "Leave our minds alone!"

Knowledge and organization I respect, and would seek to promote. I have worked conscientiously to hold back barbarism, and to advance worthy causes: racial equality, social justice, European unity, world organization, an international language.

But I have served them without fanaticism, and even, I must confess, without ardor. I have been dubbed a humanist, and I have accepted the name, with misgivings. But humanity is not self-contained: its *raison d'être* lies beyond. The perfect life on the human plane, free from disease, want, conflict, without fear, without anguish, would be that of a contented cow. *And it is not enough.*

Romantic art assigned their bounds to the Philistines, vigorous, good, and clever though they be. Their *civilization* could be justified — provided it be considered merely as a point of departure. Give us health, security, an abundance of worldly goods, and as a result freedom from care: but what shall we do with our freedom? Philistinism, however enlightened, had no answer. Beyond perfect health, perfect security, and a glut of material resources, there stretches nothing but illimitable tedium. Then art offered the renascence of wonder: either a dream world, or a magic light transforming drab reality.

Art, in the long romantic period, was associated with many causes, from reaction with Burke, Chateaubriand, and the Schlegels, to revolution with Shelley and Michelet. It never *served* any of these causes: it used them as tools or garments. For it had been the arch heresy of the Enlightenment that art, if not a mere luxury, should be a utensil. A Philosophe at his very best was a utilitarian with a deft command of language. The very essence of art, love, and religion is that they exist for their own sake only.

A short while ago, nothing could have been more *passé* than the phrase *Art for Art's Sake*. It had a stale odor of aestheticism, decadence, the Yellow Nineties, the Mauve Decade, "pink striving to be purple." James Branch Cabell, with a melancholy smile, professed to be the ultimate defender of that outmoded creed; and I, who taught it but never practiced it, felt very lonely in the grimly earnest academic world. My faith has not faltered, and I am able to speak today with greater assurance than a decade ago. We suffer from a double tyranny: the worship of meanness and greed, and the enforcement of conformity. From both, art in its purity offers to set us free. In this second part, I propose to test the validity of that promise.

Let me first nail a few theses on the door, as Luther did at Wittenberg. It is as fair and as accurate to identify Art for Art's Sake with Aubrey Beardsley or des Esseintes as it would be to equate democracy with the Dixiecrats. The philosopher of Art for Art's Sake is not James McNeil Whistler, but Immanuel Kant. The most authentic representative of Art for Art's Sake is not Oscar Wilde but William Shakespeare. If Art for Art's Sake be escape, are there not times when man's first duty is to elude the grasp of tyranny? The monks escaped from the corruption of the world; Thomas Mann escaped from Nazi oppression. The Ivory Tower is not the abode of the slothful: as in the litanies of the Virgin, it stands for "the strength there is in purity": *turris eburnea*. If the spirit of art be absolute disinterestedness and honesty, it may point the way out of our tragic confusions, social and spiritual. Science advances the same claims: but Art is human, as Science is not. The *Art of Science*, the impulse of the living scientist, is more essential than the *Science of Art*, the study of art mechanics or technique.

As I found little inspiration and less comfort in party strife and the profit motive, I felt inclined to turn from the futilities of alleged realism to the discipline and rewards of Art. But my Cartesian conscience would not allow me to call myself a devotee of Art without a searching inquiry. In the aesthetic domain as well as in the purely intellectual, our dignity should prevent us from accepting slavishly any authority or tradition. Our desire for a just government is never fully satisfied by the letter of any constitution, still less by the party machines. Religion lies deeper than the clergies, rituals, and theologies of all the sects; and in the same fashion, Art is not bound up with any doctrine, school or clique. "Artisticism" — the world ruled by and for artists — would be a "clericalism" of the most absurd kind. André Maurois's *Island of the Articoles* is a pleasing fantasy, a light satire, not a serious Utopia. It is possible to uphold the primacy of poetry without committing our souls to poet-worship. Lamartine was for a short and stormy season the

head of the French State; but I have no desire to see Mr. Ezra
Pound in the White House, although he was proclaimed by
his peers the greatest of them all. A cynic might say that Art
would be an admirable guide if it were not for the artists, just
as Communism, the doctrine and practice of the apostolic age,
would be the noblest ideal if it were not for the Communists.

So we must first brush aside a few caricatures of Art; and
it is the nature of idols to be caricatures. *Art is not erudition
about Art.* Culture is not acquired by memorizing a catalogue.
Early in this century, Wilhelm von Bode displayed in the Berlin
Museum a wax bust of Flora which he ascribed to Leonardo da
Vinci. The bust was found to be stuffed with nineteenth-century
newspapers; it was then contemptuously ejected from the temple of art. If it was indeed of such commanding quality as to
impress an expert like Bode, it should have deserved a place of
honor in any museum, with the inscription: "By an Unknown
Master." Collecting is not identical with disinterested enjoyment: Soames Forsyte was a shrewd collector. No need to over-
throw the tables of the money changers: it suffices to bear in
mind that in the courts of the temple, they are the profiteers,
not the priests. In these matters I am the merest layman: but
I note that Bernard Berenson, whose authority as an art historian is undisputed, professes the same contempt for mere
factual knowledge. The knowledge that is inspired by love and
reverence is a different affair.

Art is not technique. On the lowest level, the two words are
synonymous. In the eighteenth century, a project for the development of Paris was known as *le plan des artistes,* that is
to say of the experts or technicians. Whatever it is that you are
attempting to do, it is preferable to know how. But a clumsy
effort in the right direction is better than smooth perfection in
futilities or wrong-doing. The most subtle, intricate, and pains-
taking technique is but a dead weight if the spirit be lacking.
The tragedies and the descriptive poems of eighteenth-century
France were faultless "masterpieces" in the literal sense of the
term: they demonstrated that the authors were masters of their
craft. The Albert Memorial is technically far more ambitious and

far better finished than a humble village church. If technique be the efficient, the approved manner of manufacturing standardized objects, then art is in eternal rebellion against technique. A rebellion against all tricks of the trade, styles, patterns, *poncifs, clichés,* devised and admired by the previous generation: it became a term of reproach for a play to be called "well made," and short-story writers would blush now to end their tales with too clever a twist. A rebellion against precepts *à la* Boileau or *à la* Pope, schools, doctrines, dogmas and other machine-tools for the self-perpetuation of artistic robots. Art is the constant reassertion of the artist's freedom.

Finally, *art is not identical with artificiality.* It is a great temptation for art to spurn the obvious, even though the obvious be the unsophisticated and the natural. The conscious artist, and most of all the *would-be,* seeks salvation in defying the Philistine: art is that which Adolphe Thiers, the Prince Consort, Joseph Prudhomme, George F. Babbitt, and the indomitable Nicholas Murray Butler are not. The goats are "normalcy," the conventional, the traditional, the safe, the healthy, and even the rational: for by Cartesian definition common sense is common. The sheep are the exquisite, the rare, the precious, the decadent, the perverse, the esoteric, the cryptic, the hermetic. All this is merely the snobbishness, the Pharisaism of art, a familiar "more cultured than thou" attitude.

I gladly admit that art need not limit itself to the commonplace. Even to minds far above the average, philosophy and science are not accessible without initiation. Hegel and Einstein are frankly difficult, more difficult than Mallarmé. I condemn only the difficulty that is an opaque film concealing shallowness. At all periods, not excluding our own, there have been aspiring and yet timid souls, in mortal dread of finding themselves excluded from the inner temple. The cliques are organizations for the reassurance of the dubious. It takes a Molière to storm, or rather to laugh away, those pitiful Bastilles of Culture. The *Précieuses* easily tumble from the sublime to the ridiculous. In *The Misanthrope,* Oronte recites to Alceste a sonnet, outwardly simple by modern standards, but supposed to reveal a delicacy that only the most refined connoisseurs could appreciate. Alceste damns it in the bluntest terms, and offers as a model of true art a naïve folk song. Posterity has ratified Alceste's judgment. In art, the worst form of vulgarity is superciliousness: it is the sin against the Holy Ghost. I have adopted as the core of my ethics the maxim: "Live in such a way that you will not have to despise yourself." A grotesque deformation of that principle would be: "Take up that shibboleth that will best enable you to despise others."

In all these deviations, it is not the actual facts, but the intentions that create the difference. The true lover of art is justified in seeking erudition about the works and the artists that are precious to him. It is legitimate that he should probe fine points of technique; and he may properly refuse to be governed by "normalcy." For him, there are no forbidden paths, not even the high roads. He may happen to be a fellow-traveler with the herd, or he may venture beyond the safe-and-sane, with no certainty of finding his way back. But when sophistication is only Philistinism in reverse, when its sole aim is to astound and scandalize *épiciers* and Rotarians, then it becomes a parasite of that which it is attacking. To follow the late — and already fading — George F. Babbitt, pouring sarcasm upon him all the while, is still to be a follower of George F. Babbitt.

The cream of the jest is that, not infrequently, the Philistine is amused, and pays his jester handsomely for his antics. Whistler called Oscar Wilde a *bourgeois manqué*. But there was nothing *manqué* about Oscar; he was very successful in the bourgeois world, and coined money as well as notoriety from his pyrotechnics. His downfall was due to an aberration which had no necessary link with his art.

Some *précieux*, perverse, or esoteric writers achieved the heights of art in spite of those handicaps. They survive because of the profound simplicities manifest under their baroque frippery. The common man or bourgeois is not simple. His mind is a welter of instincts and habits, a junk shop of traditions. His speech, like his thought, is baffling because it is chaotic. Upon that tangled and writhing mass, the intuition of the great artist trains a shaft of inexorable light. In a flash, an intelligible universe is revealed. I am not a primitivist of the Rousseauistic school: truth will not be imparted to us simply because we walk on all fours. But we best recognize the power of art when it liberates us from our wearisome sophistications. There is a primitivism which is still in the forecourt of culture, and a primitivism which transcends culture. The surface opinions of Victor Hugo, from his early Legitimism to the social democracy of his old age, are commonplace enough. His clevernesses appear to us naïve or antiquated. He lives because, half concealed from us by the unique master of verbal, stagey and sentimental tricks, there was a primitive in him, and a seer of the elemental.

CHAPTER VII

John Calvin and General Booth

One thing is certain in this dubious world: no definition of art will enable us to create art. With the definition of a circle or a triangle, we can draw a recognizable circle or triangle. Given the chemical formula of a body, the raw materials, and a set of instructions, we should, with luck and care, be able to produce that body. But there is no formula, even of super-organic complexity, that will suffice to bring forth a work of art. All we can do with technical rules is to manufacture soulless forms: a "perfect" tragedy, a "faultless" sonnet. But the one thing to do with a dead sonnet is to give it prompt and deep burial: *jam foetet.*

To define art is so baffling a task that true art lovers are apt to despise theoretical aesthetics. Let pedants carp and argue: we know art when we see it, we create art when the mood is upon us. I share that prejudice: learned doctrinaires, manifestly without an inkling of the artistic spirit, writing in a style which is the very negation of art, are to me blind men discoursing about colors. Yet I cannot be satisfied with the vague. It may be that the secret of art will ever elude us: I want at least to trace a clear path right up to the gate of mystery. Above all, I do not wish tricks and shibboleths to be palmed off upon me, as though they were the very arcana of some dark life-giving faith.

For over twenty years, it was my privilege to conduct at Stanford a seminar on the Doctrine of Art for Art's Sake. It remains the pleasantest of my academic memories. The subject is inexhaustible. Every new student brought a fresh outlook, and it was fascinating also to watch the collective lights and shades that passed upon the successive waves of eager young faces. I have smiled at the Lost Generation, who, strive as they might, could not escape the California sunshine and the healthy pulse of their blood. I have wrestled with the stubbornly realistic brood midway between the two world wars. I have felt the bewilderment created by the Great Depression, and shared the anxious groping, the frustration, that darkened even the best years of the New Deal. At the very end, I have taught the returned veterans, soberly attempting to find out where they stood, and what it was they had saved. To many among them, the study of Art for Art's Sake brought neither an Open Sesame nor a surcease from mental strife, but a challenge and a touchstone.

We sought no dogma, and I discouraged the use of most treatises on theoretical aesthetics. We started with a symposium: every student wrote down, without preparation, what the word *art* actually evoked in his mind. Not a bare formula merely: but also the train of overtones and harmonics without which no thought is alive. I was not hoping for a revelation. As La Bruyère has it, men have been thinking for six thousand years, and have left nothing new to be said. But the students did attempt to discover some harmony between the ideas they had learned or devised and their innermost feelings. Not a few, in that effort, managed to give even to the most hackneyed phrase a turn that revealed the engaging freshness of their minds. In the shadow of the massive Hoover Tower, rugged individualism was our first law. If Aristotle, Plato, Kant, Schiller, Coleridge, Hegel, Rémi de Gourmont, Oscar Wilde, George Santayana, happened to agree with us, we felt gratified, but our thought remained our own.

This fundamental discussion was the most valuable part of our work. It illumined the detailed study of particular schools, periods, and authors, which formed the bulk of our work. When, as class secretary, I wrote up the consolidated minutes of the course,[1] I decided to leave out that essential introduction. It called for the conversational method, and, desiccated between

[1] *Art for Art's Sake*, Boston: Lothrop Lee & Shepard, 1936.

the leaves of a book, it would lose most of its value. I wrote it up in full for this *Bottle in the Sea*: I attempted for my own benefit to recapture the spirit of so many pleasant hours. For me, those pages could never be trite or dry, for they had the depths of many human associations. Behind almost every word, I could remember a glance, a smile, the tone of a voice. But I found that the old objection could not be overcome: the discussion remained academic. Above all, it was irrelevant to my present purpose: ignoring all scholastic subtleties, is it possible for art to provide a rule of life? [2]

The first difficulty we encounter, when we inquire into the nature of art, is that there are four faces, or four stages, denoted by the same word: the urge, the process, the material result, the response. All four are indispensable to full-rounded art, but not in the same degree. The materialists will be satisfied with the *process*, or technique, and with the *product*, or work of art. These are tangible realities. They define the field of art in the same way as ores and their transformation define the field of metallurgy. However, physical "works of art," when they reveal no inspiration and rouse no appreciation, are but lumps of clay, meaningless daubs, paper smeared with unreadable signs. They are "artifacts" without the redeeming virtue of being utensils. We are all familiar with such forms of "art," and we find little joy in them: it were better if they had never been. On the other hand, it is not impossible to by-pass the artifact. Some authorities could vouch for the authenticity of a Canaletto, yet remain indifferent to the enchantment of Venice: they are technicians, not artists. On the other hand, the man who is moved by the contemplation of a landscape, a street scene, or a human face has the essential aesthetic experience. The work of art is but the instrument, or the stimulant, which enables us to see deeper into Nature, around us and within us. We may yet learn the *art* of opening our eyes, and the *art* of closing them, without any need of the traditional gadgets.

I am aware that this is a paradox. If perverse, at any rate I

---

[2] The class was called *The Fifty-Seven Varieties of Aesthetic Experience*: rank exaggeration — we never reached half that mystic number.

am consistent in my perversity. In every field, I have come to distrust the materialists and the professionals. It seems to me that in most cases they "muscle in" and levy toll. The politicians prey on government, the profiteers prey on economic activity, the manufacturers and brokers of art goods prey on the aesthetic quest. I can imagine love without physical caresses, religion without ritual, and art without material tokens. I do not deny that the spirit may dwell, and may live more intensely, in the forms which have been specially prepared to receive it. There is religion in the churches, and most of all in the cloisters. There is art in the museums and the libraries, and most of all in the studies and the studios. What I deny is that the mechanical standardized forms are identical with the spirit. There are well-known works of art in which I find no art whatever; and there are art experiences which spurn all official vehicles. Naturally, the experts in their might will rise against me. Every professional would have us believe, and as a rule does himself believe, that his particular craft yields the very essence of our needs. Again, if you want to know what jewelry can do for mankind, be sure to consult Monsieur Josse.

These considerations lead by imperceptible degrees to a very different and far more essential problem. There is an opposition between what may be called the aristocratic conception of art and the democratic; or, as I prefer to word it, between the Calvinistic and the Salvationist. If we think of the artists as a body of men *set apart* for the production of art; if art is in our minds an activity distinct from all others; then the art world is well defined and rigorously limited. Makers, dealers, critics, connoisseurs, and even purchasers form but a small minority of mankind. This is true even of the art that comes nearest the methods of mass production and mass circulation, literature. America is a literate nation; yet, with a potential reading public of some eighty millions, few books with any claim to artistic value will sell fifty thousand copies.

Artistic production is not Big Business (the aristocrats of course must deny that the movies, television, radio music, and records have anything to do with art). Of all the things that claim the name of art, how many deserve it? Of the several thousand publications in any given year, how many are likely to survive, even for a brief season? Most books, as Rose Macaulay shrewdly remarked, "will kill time for those who like it better dead." Poems, pictures, statues, symphonies which achieve some degree of recognition are all too often accepted *faute de mieux*. Even among the works which are artistic in intent and adequate in technique, many and perhaps most are replicas, with slight variations, of a few well-established models. It is plain to us now that the French tragedies of the eighteenth century were interchangeable; but the twenty-first century is very likely to pass the same verdict on all but a handful of our novels and plays. Vast regions of "art" exist only at third hand. The public accepts art passively from the producers; the producers crib it, innocently or deliberately, from a small band of originators. *The many live on the very few.*

This aristocratic theory does not apply exclusively to art. It is obvious that, although millions are given some notions of science and may use these efficiently as practical tools, the men who are decisively increasing the field of knowledge are a consecrated and almost imperceptible minority. How much even of elementary mathematics would the average man rediscover for himself, as the child Pascal is said to have rediscovered Euclid? More paradoxically, the same has been said of love. La Rochefoucauld remarked that many would never have loved, if they had not read about it. True lovers may be as rare as Euclids, Newtons, Einsteins. The rest of us learn to love as we learn to speak our native language, which we could not have created ourselves. The souls who, unguided, have had the full religious experience might be miraculous exceptions. We repeat the words, we copy the gestures, we induce feebly a shadow of the corresponding feelings: the direct revelation, however, illumines but a few summits. Our utmost pride is to be imitators, followers, disciples.

According to this conception, the bulk of mankind is inert; even the recognized élites lack original power; the spark is found only in exceptional individuals — who may perish unknown.

This is why I called this conception Calvinistic or Jansenistic: grace is imparted only to the very small number of the elect. The rest will have to be satisfied with the reflected light, dimmer as we are farther removed from the miracle of the luminous points. For the mass, the light is not even an experience at second hand: it is at best a name.

It might be a profitable exercise in thought to out-Calvin Calvin. The elect themselves spend the greater part of their lives in darkness. For nine-tenths of their existence, poets, mystics, lovers, are Philistines like the rest of us. They should be judged by the law of the Philistine herd: decency, honesty, sanity. For nine-tenths of what is left, they carry on a desperate game of make-believe, bluffing themselves even more than the world, hoping against hope that if they strike the attitude and utter the spells of inspiration, inspiration will descend upon them. Do the gates of Heaven open magically for every believer whenever he falls on his knees? No: even the purest mystics have to fight against their own aridity, their indifference, their despair. But, miraculously, without desert, without law, a free gift of grace, inspiration, religious or artistic, does descend. So there is the saving remnant, infinitesimal and of infinite price. Two lines may sound almost alike; both may have been written primarily for effect, for profit, or for praise; yet one alone will convey the tremor. Some great poets have but half a dozen such lines in their voluminous works: yet they have not labored in vain. The haunting memory, the despairing expectancy of such moments pervade literature, carry us through countless pages of sheer sense and mere beauty. The innumerable company of readers and writers exist only for those few men, and those men only for those rare instants of illumination.

Mankind lives by the few: this conception, even if carried to its logical extreme, is far from absurd. It has at any rate the merit of traditional orthodoxy. Of the whole human race, only Noah's seed was judged worth saving. The Mohammedan world has lived for centuries on the flashes of inspiration vouchsafed to the Prophet alone. This is the *Führer* gospel in its purity: out of the seventy million Germans, the spirit of

Germany was fully manifested in Hitler and in none other. This conception underlies the common meaning of the Protean word *genius*: like grace a free gift, and precious for its extreme rarity. There are analogous cases in nature which may serve as illustrations. Who can tell? Some cosmographers hold that life such as we know it on this minute planet is a unique accident in the boundless universe. It takes tons of pitchblende to extract a few grams of radium. Aeons are required, and conditions so exacting that success seems a miracle, for carbon to be refined into a perfect diamond.

But to this Calvinistic doctrine of art, the small number of the elect, we are free to oppose the Evangelical: salvation freely offered to all men, because it is in the very nature of man to accept and receive it. As every man is potentially a saint, so is he potentially a lover, an artist, a poet. Here we meet again the antinomy we have found in Descartes: his proud solipsism: *Myself alone, and that suffices*: and his conviction that good sense is of all things the one most evenly distributed. Every man is capable of responding to the true, the beautiful, and the good: sense, taste, and conscience are the common possession of mankind. But the responses will differ, in intensity and in quality, because aptitudes are not equal, and opportunities are not alike. Before you can be attuned to a Chinese poem, you must know the Chinese language: not the characters merely, and their basic meaning, but the fullness of their implications. The degree of initiation required varies greatly. The common sense invoked by Descartes has a freer field in science than in art: material truth can be reduced to its factual and intellectual nakedness, which is universal. Aesthetic and spiritual truth cannot. In our present stage of development, we can hardly conceive of art or religion without their traditional garments, which are veils.[3]

We must at least be free to consider the hypothesis that all men feel obscurely those yearnings which are fully expressed

[3] There are great differences among the arts in this respect. It is possible to appreciate without initiation the painting and sculpture of a totally alien civilization: the power of Cro-Magnon or West African art is felt at once. Music requires an elaborate preparation. Poetry at times baffles even the erudite.

only by the few. Between the prophet and his humblest follower, there is no abyss, but a bond of brotherhood. It is the Christ within that makes us Christians; it is the divine spark in ourselves that we recognize in the historical Christ. If there were no Shakespeare in our hearts, the Elizabethan Shakespeare would be but sound and fury.

Things and concepts can be classified, at least for the sake of convenience; and they are defined by their position in the commonly accepted scheme. Not so with ultimates, such as life, love, art, religion. They can only be defined by what we may call their paradox or miracle, that is to say by their *unicity*. The paradox of art is that the unique and the common are poles asunder and yet one. Solipsism is barren: the artist who most jealously preserves his work from the desecrating glance of the public is himself, protest as he may, a social product and a social agent. The artist is inconceivable in the void: the Voice clamoring in the wilderness is heard only by the locusts. There is nothing to be said or done about the "mute inglorious Milton": he is an abstract shadowy figure. If Milton does exist for us, it is because he was vocal and achieved fame. The artist helps us most when he is most himself; but he is most himself when he feels one with the great aspirations of mankind. No one can be an "idiot," i.e., live in a private universe, and impress the world with his greatness.

These considerations, commonplace as they are, lead to strange consequences. The first is that the only true "genius," if by genius we mean the originator, the revealer, is the unknown genius. For a man's message cannot be recognized and registered until it has become fairly common. Searching scholarship brings out that every original "genius" had forerunners, dimly remembered or utterly forgotten; there is a Salomon de Caus ahead of every James Watt. These had forerunners in their turn, who escape oblivion only because they never were known. Just as Athens had an altar to the Unknown God and every capital has a shrine to the Unknown Soldier, our Pantheons ought to be dedicated in gratitude to the geniuses who did not even receive the tribute of a sneer.

The second paradox is that the genius may, in certain cases, be simply the apotheosis of the common man. "This prophet is a genius: he says exactly what I had in mind." Of these leaders who are merely floating on the surface of the stream, indicators and not causes, the clearest example is Jean-Jacques Rousseau. He woke to find himself famous, for having written a bombastic *Discourse* on an idea weary of being toyed with for ages: the vanity of a refined civilization, the greater worth of primitive simplicity. Fénelon had it in the Betica episode of his *Telemachus*. La Fontaine worked it out in his *Peasant from the Banks of the Danube*; and La Fontaine had filched the tale from Guevara. Sixteen hundred years before, it had inspired the *Germania* of Tacitus. But it happened that, at that particular time, a sufficient number of people wanted these things reasserted. Rousseauism, diffused, was ready for Rousseau. Voltaire, intelligence incarnate, could smile: "I am too old to walk on all fours." But the stampede of the Rousseauistic herd ultimately trampled down the Enlightenment.

The secret of Napoleon's greatness was his monumental commonplaceness. He was incapable of any thought or feeling beyond the range of the ordinary bourgeois. Like Monsieur Jourdain, he was a *bourgeois gentilhomme*: he craved to marry above his station. Like the average shopkeeper, he wanted two incompatible things: safety, sanity, an efficient government free from all ideological nonsense, and military glory, the romance of vulgar souls. Babbitt likewise would love to be both Calvin Coolidge and Douglas MacArthur. As a result, the Napoleonic legend is indestructible. Hitler was the common man at his worst, an accumulation of frustration, spites, and prejudices, every one of them coarse and mean, but formidable in their concentration. All three, Rousseau, Napoleon, Hitler, had the one supreme gift of egoism: they unconsciously fused their personality with their cause. Whatever increased their power was, in their eyes, for the general good. To question their intuition or their glory was blasphemy.

In art as in politics, I believe in democratic leaders, not in heaven-sent *Führer*. The word *genius* is one of those sublimities whose sole effect is to paralyze thought. I do recognize the élite within the multitude, serving, not spurning the multitude. Before such captains of the spirit, I feel at the same time humble, grateful, and free. They brought forth what I wanted said or done: without that preëxisting desire on my part, their message would be meaningless to me. They revealed me to myself — and at times I recoiled at the discovery. I feel sure that there was much in them that I could never reach; on the other hand, not one of them fully expressed my inmost depths. So my reverence remains critical. There is no artist, even the most daring, who does not at some moment strike me as irksome because conventional or shallow. There are parts of Shakespeare which are not alive to me, and no lecturing has been able to give them the vital breath. There are yearnings in me which neither Hölderlin nor Baudelaire could satisfy. The kingdom of art is both within you and among you. It is communication that brings forth consciousness; but there can be no communication unless there be, to start with, some tacit or secret correspondence.

This is the basis of what I call the Salvationist doctrine of art: redemption from the mean, freely offered to all men. I cannot hope to put it into clear intellectual terms: I must be satisfied with an adumbration. To seize upon that great promise, we must be ready to follow congenial leadership, but we must also resist enslavement. We must look beyond the sects and the cliques; we must reject and destroy the privileges of those who claim to be the sole repositories of the artistic revelation. In art as in love and in religion, professionalism is a deadly peril. We must liberate ourselves from that hero-worship which benumbs our minds and blunts our feelings. Our gratitude must be that of free men. The great books exist, not to hem us in, but to help us break our bonds.

I do not desire to eliminate art as a separate activity, and artists as a distinct body of men. But the ultimate triumph of the artistic dispensation might well entail the waning of the material work of art, and the disappearance of its maker as a special category. In the same way, democracy will find its fulfillment not in a formidable Leviathan, but in the withering of the State. When all men, released from fear and greed, are able to savor the beauty of twilight, the magic of silence, or the dawn of a smile, then they will no longer need to mess with pigments, chip a block of stone, or peddle fictitious scandal. Creation will be selection, exploration, understanding. The whole earth will be a museum and a shrine. In that far-off Utopia, the show-off and the huckster will both have been sent back to their Father. Every man worthy of the name will be a king, an artist, and a priest. And Art for Art's Sake will have full sway in the Lord's holy mountain.

CHAPTER VIII

What is art?

Portrait
of the critic as
an old man

*O*ur master Descartes counted "reviews" among the fundamental devices of his Method. In the British Parliament, all bills have to be read three times before they become law. I have no faith in mechanical reiteration. But there is a dynamic repetition which sharpens thought. It does not nail it dead with a series of hammer blows: it enables us to measure its dialectic progress. So I shall unblushingly sum up the argument, before I attempt to conclude.

In our long symposium on the nature of art, my students and I explored at least a score of theories. In this we followed Tolstoy's example, and to a large extent we accepted his guidance: after all, he was a supreme artist who had finally reached beyond art. Between his method and ours, however, there were two radical differences. The first was that we rejected none of the definitions proposed: each was to enrich the final portrait. The second is that we did not seek a single formula claiming objective validity. Only the unceasing quest is able to keep up with truth in the making.

So our first and safest finding was that there is no perfect synonym for art. Art is twenty different things, and much else besides. And these twenty different things are found also in other activities which as a rule are denied the name of art. Even their synthesis, that undefinable and potent entity we call the artistic spirit, can be discovered beyond the technical boundaries of art. There is a conscious aesthetic side to the deepest religion, to love, to war, to politics, and even to business. The balance, in many cases, is tremulous. In some of his moods, Disraeli may have used England merely as his violin; at other times, and with the utmost sincerity, he was placing all the resources of his art at the service of England. No one expressed the artistic, the sensuous delight in religion better than Milton in *Il Penseroso*. I incline to the heretical view that in his inmost depth, he was a poet rather than a Christian. A *Prometheid* might have tempted his proud and defiant spirit. Had King Arthur struck him as a more promising theme than Paradise Lost, he would have sung of Avalon instead of Eden. But the Biblical story appealed to his artistic sense because he felt it intensely — because he was a true Christian.

If I were a creative artist, I should not worry in the least about the theoretical foundations of art. A great poet or painter may hold the wrong theory, an array of conflicting theories, or no theory at all: who cares? The work is the thing. A composer may express himself in different modes and different keys, transmitted to him or created by himself: all justified, if the result be music. My own modest instrument is criticism. My single effort is to attune myself as truly as possible to all those forms of art which, in their essential notes, ring true.

So I have been a critic, attempting to train critics for the fuller enjoyment of art. But no "enjoyer," no interpreter, no critic, can be purely passive. Art demands response. At times the response may be of higher value than the stimulus. And the stimulus need not be *art* in the narrower sense: the aesthetic experience may be created by the unconscious beauty or pathos of life itself. All rituals are magic devices for evoking and materializing the spirit of a religion. They may be effective: yet it is plain that religion is immeasurably deeper than any of them. So it is in the realm of art. Works of art are but amulets and fetishes. If you believe in them, the desired result will occur: art will be manifested. But it is not they that effect the miracle by their sole virtue: they only release and focus the power latent within you.

In sorting out and arranging our rich material, I was conscious that I was simply exposing my own idiosyncrasies, which means my own blemishes. I was not attempting to teach my students my own orthodoxy, but to help them evolve their own. By orthodoxy, I meant that which was right for them, that which would give their personality more consistency and power, that which would enable them to enjoy art more fully. In the professorial chair, so easily a bastion of conformity, I remained true to the Stanford spirit. I could not brook being dictated to: so I refused to dictate. The young are accused of being rebellious: I found many to be exactly the reverse. They wanted dogmas; they were eager for servitude. Perhaps this was their rebellion against my anarchism.

The definition that emerged out of the welter was this: ART IS THE QUEST OF PLEASURE THROUGH THE CONSCIOUS EXPRESSION OF EMOTION. Five terms: every one of them indispensable. Art is a *quest*: an act of will, never a passive state. Even the casual reader cannot be carried along like a parcel: he must be a fellow-traveler. If his will falters, he drops out, and art knows him no more.

Pleasure is not limited to frivolous amusement, although amusement is not invariably contemptible. There are austere and strenuous pleasures, and pleasures which can be reached only through pain. There is sadism in the enjoyment of the noblest tragedy; and there is masochism in reading certain books which are an affliction of the spirit and a mortification of the flesh. If pleasure were totally lacking, even in the pallid form of interest, art would lose its appeal, or rather it would cease to be.

The idea of pleasure includes that of *beauty,* for beauty, whatever its character, is the sign and promise of pleasure: sensuous delight, spiritual joy, or the exhilaration of combat. Without *consciousness* there is no art. If we appreciate the charm of an object, the drama of a scene, which were not intended for our delight, then it is our awareness that is creating the art. *Expression* necessitates action upon a public. Pure thought, untouched by *emotion,* is not art. It is possible that there lurked an Edna St. Vincent Millay in Euclid, and that he quivered with joy when he looked on Beauty bare. But that is not geometry: it is poetry with a geometric background.

"Conscious pleasure in the expression of emotion" is a perfect definition for both theatricality and sentimentality. No doubt. When we condemn these as faults, it is because they are bad art, excessive, deficient, or distorted: but they are art. The loftiest poet who buttonholes us to reveal his soul to us, is dramatizing himself, feeling sorry for himself, or well pleased with himself. If he were not a poet, he would be voted a cad or a bore: no gentleman is allowed to kiss and tell. But the sole problem is: do we respond? If we do, then sentiment is transmuted into passion; the histrionic fades away; the tragic and the lyric remain in their purity.

The true work of art is not the artifact, the material instrument: it is the sense of communion, the conscious sharing of emotion. This of course defines love and religion as accurately as it does art. The kinship between the three is a basic fact. They stand so close together that at times it is hard to tell them apart; and they are distinct from all other activities. Yes, I know that there is a business side to art, that churches must have their budgets, and that lovers must finance their honeymoon trips. But such contacts are peripheral, not essential. Science, politics, economics, have their law: the forces of nature discerned and interpreted by reason. Art, love, and religion are beyond this law. Again, "the heart has its reasons that reason cannot fathom." They leave behind the realm of necessity, and dwell in the realm of grace.

The part of the critic is to serve as a liaison agent between these two realms. He will gladly follow poet, lover and mystic beyond the range of cool intelligence. But even in that exalted sphere, he cannot silence the questions: "Why?" and "How?" Man is neither pure mechanism nor pure spirit; humanism is the belief in the unity that underlies this apparent duality.

Why should we seek pleasure in the conscious expression of emotion? This takes us back to our original Cartesian position:

life (human life, the only life I know at first hand) is consciousness. If "I think, therefore I am" sounds too purely intellectual,
let us say, more lamely: "I am, because I am aware," a profundity which is a mere tautology. Absolute unconsciousness is
the perfect image of death. Blurred consciousness is a lowering
of vitality. This of course is not the biochemical definition of
life: vegetables are alive, and so is a human being in a coma.
I shall not resort to the clumsy device of "unconscious consciousness": the hypothetical soul of a turnip, the "will to live"
asserting itself obscurely in the helpless body. It is simpler to
admit that "life" has two meanings, which need not clash, but
do not coincide.

Perhaps, when we speak of *life* in connection with a book,
a cause, a nation, we are deluding ourselves with a metaphor:
the biochemist, at any rate, would have no doubt on this point.
On the other hand, it might be argued that what we call an
individual is in fact a *nation*: a cluster of material facts, interests, aspirations, held together through consciousness.
Nations and individuals may dissolve into chaos. All these meta-
phorical lives are manifestly phenomena of consciousness. A
book of which no one is conscious — not even its author — is
not alive. If no one were conscious of being a Christian,
Christianity would be dead. If all men ceased to believe in the
existence of the United States, the United States would no
longer exist. It is not a territory that makes a nation. The Congo
Free State never came to life; Poland, torn asunder for over a
century, kept breathing, a remorse and a hope, in the consciousness of mankind.

We are not merely, like the plants and the brutes, struggling
for survival against our fellow creatures: man has long ago
transcended Darwinism. What we are fighting is annihilation.
It yawns beneath us, and our consciousness of life is our only
way of clutching reality. More pressing even than the fear of
physical death is the dread of that "death in life," the loss of our
identity. On the lowest plane, hunger, on the middle ground,
politics and economics, on the highest level, science and certain
brands of philosophy, all would reduce us to mere inter-

changeable units, swayed by irresistible laws. The man who
starves is no longer a man, he is an aching organism, one with
the brutes. The man whose every step is determined is no longer
a man, he is a cog. Art leads the fight against the material, the
statistical, the mechanical, which assail us on every side and
would rob us of our selfhood. The sense of liberty and the sense
of life are one.[1]

Pater's promise: "to give the highest value to your moments
as they pass," and St. John's: "I am come that they might have
life, and that they might have it more abundantly," are answers
to the same cry of anguish: "Do not let me die!" Art, love, and
religion respond to that basic need. They are not identical, but
they coöperate in the same way as, in the other sphere, science,
industry, commerce, and government work — or should work
— in the closest harmony.

When I make this distinction between the two spheres, it
is in no Manichean spirit. I do not consider the material, the
statistical, the mechanical as essentially evil. If they check
hunger, disease and fear, they remove obstacles in the ascent
to the higher freedom. Their one justification is to relieve us
from worldly care. If on the contrary they increase our care, if
they absorb our energy, if they restrict the scope of art, love,
and religion, then they dull our consciousness of life, they lower
our human quality, they are instruments of death, servants
strangling their masters.

Art then is that which enhances our consciousness. That is
why the great themes of art are love and death, the hope and the
dread which are the poles of our being. Everything that quickens
life — all forms of play, the great games of business, politics,
and war, the adventure of research and discovery, fulfills the
essential purpose of art. A victory in any field reassures us as to
our own existence. What distinguishes art is that art is the
most direct form of self-assertion. Art is licensed, and even
glorified, egotism. It is also the most accessible: if you select

---

[1] Art is thus in scrupulous agreement with the wisdom of the Founders:
it helps to secure and expand our inalienable rights, life, liberty, and
the pursuit of happiness.

the Stock Exchange or the Senate as your instruments, you will find them exacting, expensive, and uncertain. It is much simpler to write a sonnet. And the sonnet may outlive the Senatorial term, the Senator, even the Senate itself: "robust art alone possesses eternity."

Art is the domain of pure freedom. There are strict rules to the game, even if you are playing it with yourself alone: Solitaire is no fun if you cheat. But you can at will pick out or devise a different game; at will also, you can refuse to play. In his own world, the artist is sovereign. If he abdicates, if he hires himself, he is no longer an artist. Pure freedom includes freedom from responsibility. In this respect, art stands unique. The material world is an unbreakable chain of obligations. In love, you pledge yourself to another. If you accept religion, your life is bound by a law. When the artist, like Ezra Pound, ventures into the alien field of politics, he is fair game for his political enemies: free verse offers no sanctuary. But if he remains scrupulously on artistic ground, he cannot be held to account.

As a result of this freedom, art is *safe*. For art is experience imagined, reflected, recollected, not experience in the raw. So it is able to provide exhilaration without peril. Art is like the roller coasters in our amusement parks: it offers us vertiginous plunges, breath-taking curves, impending catastrophes —all with the firm assurance that within a few moments, you will be on solid ground again. Through art, we can cheerfully enter the Gate that bids us leave every hope behind. Through art, we can afford to sport with a tigress like Valérie Marneffe: [2] the bars between her and our world will not break.

Art is the willing suspension of disbelief: tersely and bluntly, art is make-believe: "Let us pretend. . ." This does not mean that art is frivolous and immoral, and that poets, wreathed with flowers, should be banished from our Puritan Republic. Art does contain large elements of reality, direct or transposed; it has a consistency of its own, which can be harmonized with pure logic. Else it would not be convincing; it would not "suspend

[2] In Balzac's *Cousin Betty*.

disbelief," and therefore it would not be enjoyable. But its goal, whatever the Realists and Naturalists may say, never is "the humble truth": it is the truth arranged for our pleasure. Art has its uses, besides killing time. It offers an excellent education for life; it deepens our consciousness; it sharpens our vision. It can serve as a warning: nothing that is artistically wrong can be wholly good or wholly true. Still, no true lover of art would reduce it to pedagogy. Art is hypothesis, exploration, experiment, blue-printing, an optimistic or pessimistic Utopia: yet even this is a by-product. We enjoy a poem or a statue without any thought that ultimately they will contribute to a practical reform. Art has nothing to offer but enhancing our consciousness of life. What to do with our life is a different problem.

Every great cause has in it some element of great art: imagination, sympathy, the creative urge, the desire to shape human conditions into a more harmonious mold, the vigorous assertion of personality. But no worthy cause is pure art, and pure art serves no cause. It is a primary condition of honest thinking that we should draw the line, however sinuous and shadowy, between the two. Santayana sang:

> I sought on earth a garden of delight,
> Or island altar to the Sea and Air,
> Where gentle music were accounted prayer,
> And reason, veiled, performed the happy rite.

But reason spurns a veil; religion is stern and will not be satisfied with gentle music.

The story is told — the tone is Renan's, but I am not sure — of a preacher who drew tears from his congregation by describing the sufferings of Christ. His heart smote him when he beheld their bitter sorrow, and he sought to comfort them with these words: "My little children, do not weep so hard. All this happened a long time ago. And perhaps it is not quite true." Here is the crux. Of every event, doctrine, legend, or myth, Sakyamuni, Prometheus, bound or unbound, Job, Dante's other world, Milton's epic of rebellion, downfall, and hope, Goethe's Faust, we have the right to ask: "To what degree and in what sense is it true?"

Art makes us realize that there is a domain beyond mere fact and mere thought. But is this domain mere delight, accepting no responsibility, offering no guidance? Or is there a third realm beyond? I said repeatedly that science, through the study of "race, environment, and time," for instance, or through psycho-physiology, could lead us to the threshold of art, but had no access therein. In the same way, art leads us to the very portal of religion, but cannot enter the fane. Art and religion are allies against materialistic science: but alliance for a definite purpose implies no identity. In order to understand religion in its austere purity, we must examine and allow the fullest claims of art — and then leave them resolutely behind. We must above all purge religion from everything that is not belief, but mere suspension of disbelief, everything that is valid only on the artistic plane. The gods of Olympus, the Walhalla of Wagner, Santa Claus, are "made up," and we know it. The storied windows richly dight, the pealing organ, the full-voiced quire, are no argument: they could be placed at the service of idols. A Nazi festival was infinitely more impressive than a Quaker meeting. *Let us not pretend.* The quest of pleasure through the conscious expression of emotion is not religion.

@hips from the workshop

Most of the problems discussed in my course on *Art for Art's Sake,* at Harvard, Brandeis, and particularly at Stanford, will be found in my book by the same title, the consolidated report of a long inquiry. Hundreds of essays on "An Artistic Utopia," the blue-prints of the society most favorable to the flowering of art, passed through my hands. They were condensed in two essays, reprinted as two chapters, "A Utopia for Literature," and "Literature in Utopia," in my book *Literature and Society.* I am appending two oddities hitherto uncollected.

The first was entitled "God as an Artist," an idea which will be familiar to readers of Chateaubriand, Ruskin, Anatole France, and James Branch Cabell. It might have been called "A Theological Fantasy on a Definition of Art." It never was written out in full. Here is the argument in barest outline.

God created the world. Why? Was He not perfect? He created the world as a mode of self-realization, of self-expression. Self does not exist without the Non-Self, or other selves. Before the world was created, God was (strictly: God *is*); but there was no personal God, only a "mute inglorious God."

God took pleasure in His creation: "And He saw that it was good." After a final survey, this approval was reiterated: "And God saw everything that He had made, and behold, it was very good." Later, He repented, and wanted to destroy the work of His own hands. These alternations of elation and despair are part of the artistic (poetic or creative) temperament. More coolly critical, we think that the Supreme Artificer was too easily satisfied. The world was not so very good after all, for it included the Serpent. But it was, according to Leibniz and Rousseau, the best He could do.

Why did God create us? To His own glory: that we should
worship Him and magnify Him. In human words, we are His
public.

Fashioned after God's image, we too seek realization through
creation. We too look upon our work and see that it is good;
although we too may soon be sorely tempted to destroy it, as
Kleist, Gogol, Kafka, did or wanted to do. We too desire a
public that will magnify us, enhancing thereby our sense of our
own existence. Like God, we create a public after our own
image. We seek to gather together like-minded men, if such do
exist; or to impose upon others a mind like unto our own. Art,
from the first artifact, which is the world, to the latest poem,
can be defined as "the instrumentality whereby we create for
ourselves a public of worshippers."

The other oddity is "An Aesthetic Decalogue." Of this also,
hundreds of specimens passed through my hands. I am offering
only a composite picture, not so sharp as many of its components. The problem was not to formulate the ten major rules
of Art. Nor was it — this was a sore temptation — merely to
transpose the Biblical Decalogue into artistic terms: the result
of such an attempt was invariably a parody, smart and insincere.
The problem was to formulate ten rules of conduct, on the
hypothesis that great art and the good life are inseparable.

THE LAW OF THE IVORY TOWER
DECALOGUE OF ART FOR ART'S SAKE

I. Thou shalt love Beauty with all thy heart, and serve her
in every way.

II. Beware of false gods: the ugly may be true, but it cannot
be good.

III. Thou shalt make unto thyself graven images, and rejoice
in them; for this is the outward service of Beauty.

IV. Take thought for the morrow, for art is long, and the moment is fleeting.

(*vulgo*: beware of the hangover: it is inartistic. If thou wouldst tell a good tale, be sure to live to tell the tale.)

V. Make thyself free from worldly care; else thou canst not serve Beauty with a single heart.

Comment: four ways:

a. asceticism

b. parasitism (Harold Skimpole: "Let Martha do it!").

c. parallelism: secure leisure, and use it well.

d. professionalism: do what thy heart desires, and be paid for it.

VI. In the house of Art there are many mansions; be not over-ready to call thy brother: "Thou Philistine!"

VII. Be free, and respect freedom: even Beauty imposed upon others turns to ugliness.

VIII. Whatever ugliness thou inflictest upon thy brother, it shall reach unto thy very soul.

IX. Beauty is more than skin-deep. (Not ornament merely but structure; not paint, but health; not cleverness, but sincerity.) The ugliness of thine inmost heart will destroy the beauty of thy face. (*Dorian Gray.*)

X. Shut out the hubbub of Vanity Fair, and hearken unto the still stern voice of Taste, and thou shalt do nothing base.

PART III

Faith

Faith is the Hope
that Charity is not vain.

CHAPTER IX

The metaphysical god

$\mathcal{M}$etaphysics and theology are not merely inseparable; they are, over a vast area, identical. A religion may start with an immense hope, a desire for a purer, more ardent life, and its central point may be the concrete example of a great leader: but inevitably the teachings are organized into a metaphysical system. Even the least philosophical of religions, the barest theisms, Judaism and Mohammedanism, have evolved their theologies. Conversely, there is no metaphysics, however stark, abstract, free from historical associations, divorced from any ritual or hierarchy, that is not at least the skeleton of a religion. Even Spinoza's rigid geometry is a revelation of the divine.

What is the place of metaphysics in our religion, that is to say in our inmost life? In this inquiry, I am faced at the outset with a formidable obstacle: I am appalled at my own presumption. The method discussed in the first part of this book may be summed up in a single word: honesty. Faith we must have, if our spirit is to keep alive; but it must be faith without fear or favor, free from delusion, free from pretense. Never proclaim, never accept a thing as true unless it appears to you clearly and evidently to be such. This Cartesian test, by the way, brings out the line of cleavage between theology and metaphysics. In theology, there must be, at some point, a surrender, an abdication: question no further; fall down on your knees and adore. In metaphysics, every philosopher starts with a ruthless critique of all previous systems. It is not sacrilegious for a philosopher to reject Plato or Spinoza, Kant, Hegel, or Comte. He would not be worth his salt if he were not prepared, like the priest of Nemi, to slay his predecessor. There is no thinking at second hand. Whoever does not reject all previous authorities is at best a historian, a scholiast, or an eclecticist: he is no philosopher.

But if the rejection of one system after another is the very life of philosophy, the rejection of all systems — even skepticism, even empiricism — is still held to be a blasphemous and futile paradox. For such rejection implies that the enormous mental fabrics erected by the titans of thought were, in the last analysis, vanity: wells without water, pits without ore, splendid porticoes opening on the inane. Before such a sweeping negation, the freest mind cannot repress misgivings which verge upon dread. It cannot be so easy: to shrug away the giants argues yourself a fool. Madame de Staël peremptorily demanded of the German philosophers that they give her in ten minutes the gist of their system. When they demurred, she flashed back: "Whatever cannot be made clear to me in ten minutes is not worth understanding." And the negator does not grant them even those ten minutes of grace: they are sentenced before they have opened their lips. A philosopher has the right to demolish the system of another philosopher, because he devotes his whole life to philosophical thought, and admits the essential validity of philosophy. But a layman who dismisses all systems and calls metaphysics a blind alley seems like a high school sophomore shaking his head at Einstein.

Yet there are differences. Science is cumulative: many theories die, many experiments once thought decisive are found incomplete and faulty; still, there is a constant accretion to the vast body of organized knowledge. And scientific truth must be demonstrable: no hypothesis achieves the (precarious) dignity of a law until it has stood that practical test. The innumerable systems of the metaphysicians have never thus cohered into a consistent whole. Each new philosophy is a world apart, following a course of its own in the uncharted void. Not one of them is capable of practical demonstration. More: not one can be established beyond doubt even in the domain of pure theory. The best systems may be faultless exercises in formal logic, free from inner contradictions: but at the core there always is an assumption that is gratuitous, a flight of imagination, an act of faith. There always is a pathetic attempt to catch the absolute in the mesh of human words. And the ultimate words are confessedly devoid of sense. They explain, but cannot be explained; they embrace all, but are beyond comprehension. The absolute, the infinite, the eternal, are not actual conceptions, with a definite meaning: they are mere denials of the wall which encompasses us. We live and move and have our being in a world hemmed in by space, time, causality. It is elementary wisdom to recognize that these limitations do not define or confine the universe. I cannot shake off my bonds: but I know that they are bonds. That which falls under our senses, that which is reconstructed or freely constructed in our minds cannot be all. It is indeed but an infinitesimal part of the ultimate reality. Materialistic science is only picking up pebbles by the seashore; the most subtle and rigorous logic is only arranging these pebbles into patterns that please us with their symmetry. It is part of man's dignity to know that he is in prison, to acknowledge the boundless mystery that surrounds him; it is part of his laughable infirmity to dream of capturing that mystery with his puny hands and his puny brains.

Through the ages, philosophers have attempted their Indian rope trick: climbing out of sight on a rope they had themselves flung into the air. Through the ages, while masses stood agape, wise men shrugged their shoulders. For the condemnation of the attempt is as old as the attempt itself. It was not Victorian encyclopedists like Thomas Huxley and Herbert Spencer who created *agnosticism* and *the unknowable*, i.e., the sense of mystery. The thought is found in the Book of Job, in Greek tragedy, in the poets and mystics of all times, in the dark Orphic wisdom of Goethe, in the blind unconquerable gropings of the later Hugo, in the flutey yet solemn melody of *In Memoriam*. We find that thought at the two poles of French literature: Voltaire wrestling with the problem raised by the disaster of Lisbon; Pascal, scientist and mystic, wit and logician, struck with terror at "the eternal silence of infinite space," and concluding: "True philosophy laughs at philosophy."

The refusal to accept the validity of all human philosophy is exactly the reverse of arrogance: it is sincere humility. The men who are drunk with pride are those who dream of erecting a Babel that will reach unto the very heaven. Bulk, elaborateness, impressiveness, are no arguments. It is magnificent, but it is not wisdom. But I do not consider myself in any way superior to the men who have worked so hard, even though it was against sense and against hope. We men of the twentieth century have long rejected Greek mythology, but we do not feel that we have risen above the Greeks, whose faith was linked with so many masterpieces. We hold ourselves justified in declining to hack a path through the dense jungle of Hindu philosophy: yet we acknowledge its greatness. We are indifferent to the extreme subtleties of the Scholastic philosophers: but we recognize in that school of thought an effort matching those of the Greeks and of the Germans.

So I am not lacking in reverence for the great metaphysicians and the great theologians of the past. Great systems are great poems, stripped of all vain ornament, functional and not baroque; masterpieces of rigorous technique, expressions of unique and powerful personalities. But the actual knowledge they yield is scrupulously nil. It is possible to admire the *Summa* and the *Divine Comedy*, *Paradise Lost* and Spinoza's *Ethics*, to find in them not aesthetic pleasure merely, but stimulation and sustenance, without accepting them in the least as literal revelations of objective truth. I feel modest, not merely before the great figures of the past, but before my younger contemporaries. I recognize the erudition, the subtlety and cogency of thought, the power of expression, above all the manifest good will of men like Gilson, Maritain, Barth, Niebuhr, Buber, Clarence Macartney, and, in fields closely related to theology, of T. S. Eliot and Arnold Toynbee. They are my superiors, but they are not my masters, any more than Karl Marx, who is no less learned than they, no less logical, no less forcible, no less devoted to the betterment of man's fate. It is possible for rejection to be free from contempt, and even to be tinged with sympathy.

But this admiration only intensifies my regrets. The pity of it! These powerful lights probing the infinite have not made a perceptible dent into its impenetrable darkness. They attempt to scale *and desecrate* the absolute, and the result is a house of words. Some Hindus believe that the earth rests upon the back of an elephant, and that the elephant himself stands on a tortoise. But what supports the tortoise? Ah! Inquire no further: that secret is beyond the reach of the human mind. I can easily spare the elephant and the tortoise, and their elaborate measurements, and the vivid colors with which they are depicted. I am able to enjoy mythological animals, like the White Whale in *Moby Dick* or the Octopus in *Toilers of the Sea*, because they do not demand literal belief. An uncreated Creator, a First Cause without cause, a Prime Mover without motion, are on a level with the elephant and the tortoise. They do not explain: they exist on a painted screen rigged up between our experience and the unfathomable. In the meantime, while powerful minds are engaged in this phantasmagoria, there are pressing soluble problems, war and want, disease and madness, that are loftily ignored, or too often turned over to the huckster and the hack. Our appointed leaders are betraying us for a handful of abstractions.

Discourse is melodic, while thought should be, and is, symphonic. I have just spoken like a utilitarian, an empiricist, a contemner of pure thought, eager only for usable truths that will promote the welfare of mankind. My words, if so interpreted, were but a travesty of my mind. I am not satisfied with the practical plane. I do not admit for a moment that our world of senses and sense is the whole of the universe, or even gives a true picture of the minute part of the cosmos that immediately surrounds us. I accept the possibility of miracles, not as scientific facts previously unobserved, not as mere coincidences, but as a definite and deliberate interference of another plane of existence with our own. I am ready to see the heavens roll up like a scroll. I accept even a miracle greater than any suspension or alteration of material law: the mystic experience, a force beyond our human ken singling out one of us, and speaking to him secrets which human tongue can not utter. My quarrel with theologians and metaphysicians is that they are not mystics: they are logicians. They are using the instruments of reason, effective and almost infallible in their proper sphere, in a domain that reason cannot reach. We need poets, to awaken and intensify our sense of mystery, awe and wonder; we need scientists, to guide our steps in a world of physical phenomena. Metaphysicians are both and neither. They lose themselves in a world of pretentious shadows, the mere projection of our earthly conditions upon the blank impenetrable veil of the unknown.

Yet I can see the use of metaphysics, at one stage in human development. Primitive man (and rare among us are those who are not primitive) casts his hope and dread in the form of myths, which, objectified, become idolatrous superstitions. Metaphysics works upon those myths; purges away their manifest grossness; makes them aseptic, innocuous. It drives away the spirits, malign or kindly, lurking in every glade, crag or river, and leaves only principles, laws, ultimately a single supreme Law. But these laws are the lingering diaphanous wraiths of ancient idols. "Nature," "Energy," "Law" itself, are conceived as entities, endowed with a will. The last effort is for the metaphysical age to transcend itself, to refine itself out of existence. The myth that is an abstraction has killed the myth that was spurious knowledge, i.e., superstition. Now the abstraction itself must die, or survive as the merest tool. This will release the myth, closer perhaps to the primitive than to the metaphysical, that is prospective, an aspiration, not false science or false history; the myth that is truly spiritual, because we are conscious that it is not objective truth; "the Christ that is to be," hailed, in what we are pleased to call the murk of the Victorian age, by Alfred Lord Tennyson.

Professional metaphysicians are but a handful: I wonder how many professors of philosophy have a metaphysical system of their own. Yet the evil they do is immeasurable. For they have transmitted to the theologians, and the theologians to the defenseless masses, the idea or idol of the Metaphysical God: the abstraction of abstractions, the Being that is not a being, but all being; the sum total of negations, Absolute, Eternal, Infinite.

Such a God is the apex of thought, and annihilates thought. It is impossible to conceive a part of the universe where He is not, that is not His, that is not He. The Metaphysical God cannot stop short of Pantheism, and Pantheism destroys any conception of good and evil, all things being absolutely and equally divine. I defy any man to derive comfort, guidance, or hope from a God identical with every particle of the universe, a God who is one with the food and the poison, one with the slayer and the slain. Such a God is but logic gone mad, and relentlessly grinding thought into inanity. But by jerking us constantly between the Living God, the God who is a leader, a friend, a father, and the God that is the Absolute, metaphysical theology ruins, on the human plane, the integrity of our minds. It introduces into our thought the most corrosive element: the Absurd that refuses to confess its own absurdity. All Western religions are theistic, and consider Pantheism as a yawning gulf. Yet they also speak of God in those negative terms — Absolute, Infinite, Eternal — which leave no room except for Pantheism. In terms of human experience, Pantheism and atheism are one.

CHAPTER X

The living god

With Pascal then I reject "the god of the philosophers," the $x = \infty$ annihilating thought, purpose, action. I want a God who gives meaning to my life, a Living God.

That God is a leader. We are under his banner. He claims, and will reward, our loyalty. He has a purpose, which in our humble sphere we serve. He has a will, and to be one with that will is the secret of peace. He crushes the rebel, he chastises the traitor, he rebukes the sluggard, he praises the faithful. A stern disciplinarian, he is not inexorable. He has mercy on the broken reed and the smoking flax. He is a commander in supreme control, but he is also a father. With this conception, our duty becomes plain, and the riddles of the moral universe disappear. We may be mired, we may be tortured, our lives may be sacrificed to ends which we cannot see. But these are insignificant skirmishes in the fight that fills the cosmos. We shall share in his final triumph, and live under his beneficent rule forever.

This conception is human, dramatic, and above all, moral. It gives *sense*, i.e., direction, purpose, to our obscure striving. Without it the world would be a soulless mechanism, or else sheer chaos. It is the basis of all dynamic religions. But we must be aware of its ineluctable implications.

The first, I repeat, is the rejection of the Infinite Metaphysical God. A living God works and suffers as we do; he is capable of anger, tenderness, and even repentance. He is not the absolute: he is our chief and our comforter. He is *personal*, which means that he has limits. He has to struggle to establish and maintain his kingdom. You cannot have at the same time such a God, and the abstraction of Pantheism. Those who attempt to keep the two conceptions present in their minds, and under the same name, are simply afraid of their own thought. They are bowing to the great idol Muddleheadedness.

A living God is a fighting God. Who and what are his enemies? A curious conception is found in ancient Greece, in Jean-Jacques Rousseau, and in our days among certain "liberal" Christians. God is a person: the enemy is not. God is struggling, along with us, and for us, against conditions not of his own making. Above Prometheus there was Jupiter; but above Jupiter there was Fate. Not a person, not a purpose, but an inexorable power, blind to human suffering, deaf to human prayers. God is leading the rebellion against that crushing yoke, challenges its contemptuous silence. When Voltaire wondered how an all-wise, all-powerful Providence could tolerate, could have conceived, could have created evil, Rousseau, in the name of Leibniz and Pope, made answer: "Man, be patient; evils are a necessary effect of the nature and constitution of this universe. The eternal and beneficent Being who governs it would have liked to spare thee all these sufferings; of all possible arrangements (*économies*) he has selected the one which combines the least amount of evil and the greatest amount of good; or, if we must speak even more crudely, if he has not done better, it is because he could not do better." [1]

Thus the loving kindness of Providence is saved, but it is at the expense of God's omnipotence. God *rules* the universe, but under conditions for which he is not responsible, some of which are definitely evil in his sight: just as the pioneer who clears and tills the land has to take for granted the configuration, the soil, the climate. God is intelligent energy struggling against forces wholly indifferent to man. This is an ancient and ubiquitous thought. In modern times, it was the core of Napoleon's creed: he, the incarnation of will-power, acknowledged necessity, destiny, "the force of things," as the ultimate realities. We can thread our precarious way only through the crevices of destiny: at any moment, the crevices may close. We find the

[1] Letter to Voltaire, August 18, 1756.

same thought in Alfred de Vigny, whose "God of Ideas" is at war with implacable Nature. It reappears in Albert Camus, for whom the universe is "absurd," not existing for the benefit of the human race, not following the laws of human reason.

But if we objectify the forces serving what we call *good*, it is almost inevitable to objectify also the forces of evil. Manicheism, although under that name it was but an obscure heresy, is implicit in every living theism. The lines are drawn: there is good and there is evil, there is right and there is wrong, there is light and there is darkness, and we must choose our side. The battle is no mere shadow fight: the issue must be dubious, else God would merely be playing a cruel and futile comedy at our expense. He has not crushed the devil yet because so far he has not been able to. Indeed, those who believe in an eternal hell admit that the struggle will end, not in total victory, but in a stabilization of the front. Satan will forever rule over his own, whom God could not snatch away from him. According to John Calvin, Satan's flock will be by far the larger. According to the unknown author of *Aucassin and Nicolette*, it will be the more attractive as well.[2]

The two conceptions, the Fighting God and the Omnipotent God, constantly clash in our minds and confuse our thinking. If we accept the Fighting God, the scheme of redemption becomes intelligible. God has suffered a set back in the Holy War, when Satan successfully tempted man into disobedience. This loss had to be retrieved: Christ came to buy back (*redeem*) man from the clutches of Satan. It was to Satan then that the sacrifice on the cross was offered. According to Crane Brinton, this idea of ransom from the enemy satisfied the early Fathers and was accepted for centuries. "But to subtler minds, such ransom

---

[2] Manicheism has left deep traces in thought and in literature. The power of Satan was awe-inspiring, and his wiles hard to resist. Not a few truckled with him for immediate advantages, down to Thomas Mann's *Dr. Faustus*. Others, not for selfish gain, and with open eyes, went over to the opposition, because they thought Satan had been wronged. Cf. Blake (who tried to enlist Milton in the Devil's party, "like all true poets"), Byron, Vigny, Baudelaire, Carducci. The ultimate reconciliation of the two principles has been treated by two writers of very unequal stature, Victor Hugo in *The End of Satan*, Marie Corelli in *The Sorrows of Satan*.

seemed almost a commercial transaction; moreover, it put God in a position unworthy of his omnipotence and dignity." [3] So we must have it that God sacrificed himself to himself, according to a plan he had conceived of all eternity: it is inconceivable that the Absolute God should fight a battle, and a losing battle at that. But then the splendid and profound stories of Fall and Redemption become meaningless. The mission of Christ, the passion of Christ, the victory of Christ, lose their reality; they become part of Maya, the delusion that veils for us the eternal world.

If we probe our hearts, we find that the living God, the fighting God, the invisible King, is the only one that has any meaning for us. When we invoke, for the sake of superficial logic, the metaphysical abstraction we call God, it only creates confusion in our minds and hearts. When it comes to action, the difference between the two is even more radical. God the leader demands unquestioning obedience: but that obedience is active, and in response to definite orders. It is a rule of life. The abstract God cannot command and cannot be obeyed, since he is all in all. For the pawns he pushes about in his eternal game with himself, the only possible attitude is one of utter passivity.

For most believers, the conception of the Fighting God is frankly anthropomorphic. He is the leader of *mankind*. He fashioned us in his own image; and the enemies, the rebellious angels, also bear a human countenance, originally, like ours, divine, today distorted and debased, but still recognizable. This pure anthropomorphism is not inevitable. Just as we are wrestling with "fiends in human shape," we may find on our side spirits of light in the semblance of animals: the lion and the eagle, the lamb and the dove. Even the ass, symbol of Dostoevsky's *insulted and injured*, may be illuminated by a ray of divine effulgence: Balaam's mount saw the angel when the prophet was still blind. Hugo, in his great poem *The Toad*, makes the ass the vessel of divine pity. Conversely, Melville's Moby Dick, and the octopus in *Toilers of the Sea*, are incarnations of the evil principle. The human shape may be only one of our in-

[3] Crane Brinton, *Ideas and Men* (New York, 1950), p. 194.

numerable avatars. Hugo denied the gulf between animate and inanimate: according to "the Mouth of Darkness," everything in the universe is alive, and full of souls. The stone suffers in stoic silence for the crimes of a previous existence; the flame writhes in despair or aspiration. The purely anthropomorphic view is a thin and narrow pseudo-rationalism, afraid of the grotesque and of the ludicrous. The teeming mythologies of the primitives and the somber visions of modern poets are more adequate symbols. The hero of the cosmic drama is Life, not merely human life; thought goes beyond human syllogisms; love, beyond human words.

Anthropomorphism, which plays such a large part in the Judaic and Christian faiths, reached its purest manifestation in the first half of the last century. It has been variously called Romantic Democracy, the cult of Humanity, Prometheism, the New Christianity, the religion of 1848. It arose when the Romantic spirit had won its revolt against the cool rationality of the Enlightenment, and had freed itself from the Toryism of Burke, de Maistre, the Schlegels, Chateaubriand. It had great prophets in France: Lamennais, Lamartine, Hugo, Michelet; and from their works a potent *Bible of Mankind* could be compiled. It had a philosophy, shot through with bewildering Utopian flights; it even had a church, with the master of Auguste Comte, the crack-brained bohemian and genius Henri de Saint-Simon.

Mankind is the collective incarnation of the divine: such is the central dogma of this faith. Nothing could be more orthodox; for we were taught that God fashioned us in his own image, and breathed his spirit into our clay. The service of mankind and the service of God are therefore one and the same. Brotherhood is a fact, and fraternity a duty. The perfect man, the essence and symbol of mankind, the Son of Man, is *ipso facto* the Son of God par excellence. Lamartine translated: "The Word was made flesh" as "The Word is made Humanity." It is only by communing with the whole of humanity that we can reach the Father. Romanticism has often been defined as the hypertrophy of the ego: yet at this point it merges with Pascal's thought: the

Ego is hateful. Self is sin; property is theft; individualism is damnation. "O fool!" declares Hugo, "who dost not know that I am thou!"

A refinement in this anthropotheology came with the growth of the historical spirit, the Hegelian sense of becoming, the all-embracing doctrine of evolution. God himself is emerging within the collective consciousness of mankind. As mankind realizes its divine character, it shapes itself into God. This God in the making will never be achieved: it is the process that is divine. There is a *sense* in the universe: whatever hampers the progress of God is evil. Such a God is not finite, not a "magnified non-natural man"; but he is not identical with the whole of the universe, like the abstract God of the pantheists. He is conquering, he is creating the world as he goes.

The first dawn of mankind's divine nature came with the Fall: *felix culpa!* The tempter made a promise which can never be fulfilled, but which started man on his endless quest: "Ye shall be like gods." But this consciousness implied a rebellion against the unreasoning, the brutish acceptance of the Edenic world. That revolt was a wrench, a break, a "fault." Man had, and still has, obscure torturing misgivings about that fateful step. He hankers for the peace of innocence, as the child is said to hanker for the shelter of the womb. Man is still feeling the anguish of his spiritual birth. Christ came to bring reassurance: man should lay aside his terrors, and strive to be perfect, as his Father in heaven is perfect. Such a Heaven, God's kingdom, is not "of this world," that is to say not "of this time." It is both within us, and ahead of us. We are building it, here and now, in our own hearts; but it will never be completed within the range of human time. When the king and the kingdom have reached perfection, when mankind and God are one — "a divine far off event" — then time will cease to be. This "God in the making" was the object of faith of men very different from Lamennais or Hugo: Ernest Renan, Henri Bergson, André Gide.

In terms of eternity — quoting again the immortal Monsieur de la Palisse — time vanishes (and space with it: for space is measured by time. If we could be *instantaneously* anywhere, distance would be annihilated). The dynamic conception exists in time: time is of its essence. And if there is *sense*, i.e., direction, in this God-creating quest, there is progress. Here many thinkers balk. Progress is thoroughly unpopular with the refined, because it is all too popular with the herd. As we have seen it is associated with the mental intoxication, the rash promises of the Enlightenment; followed by a second, heavier, more turbid wave during the materialistic age. We damn progress, because its prophets announced the millennium near at hand. They had led us to expect that its course would be uninterrupted; and now we see relapses into abysmal depths of superstitions and cruelties. If Condorcet prophesied a "kingdom of Progress" in his own generation, he erred tragically; just as Jesus erred, according to Reinhold Niebuhr and Albert Schweitzer, when he thought that his kingdom was at hand, that some of his disciples would never know death. In both cases, the timetable was erroneous; in neither is the goal disproved.

The fallacy is to confound progress with a static Utopia. Because we did not reach "Progress" by 1800, it is taken for granted that progress is a fraud. But you cannot *reach* progress: you can only reach for it, and by so doing live it. Obviously the obstacles were greater than the pioneers imagined. Condorcet could not have foreseen that a century and a half after his death, educated men, turning their back on the Enlightenment, would deliberately and proudly choose darkness. But above all, progress is eternal discontent. Only the unprogressive look backward and smile complacently at their advance: "Fifty years of ever-expanding commerce!" The progressive mind forges ahead faster than events can follow; so it discovers more ills than it is able to cure. Faith in progress is an impatience that borders on despair.

It must never be forgotten that the Fighting God, the God of creative evolution, is not a dogma but a myth. History unrolls *as if* an increasing purpose — an increasing consciousness of purpose — were at work within it. An *as if* never is an explanation, even though, to create the proper sense of profundity, we should call it *als ob*. Naturally, the myth tallies with the course of history as you see it, since you have made the myth for that very end. I am quite willing to admit that the French armies of 1792 rushed to battle *as if* the Spirit of the Revolution were hovering over them, singing the *Marseillaise*: I admire the magnificent statuary of Rude on the Arch of Triumph. But the figure was created to represent the event, it did not shape the event. The fighting soul of revolutionary France, the Fighting God our king throughout the ages, are more dynamic symbols than the elephant and the tortoise; but as metaphysical, as theological explanations, they are just as irrelevant. As works of art, on the contrary, they may be of supreme significance. For they create in us, on a plane different from reality, the mood which, transposed, will enable us to face and reshape reality. That is why art is real, while metaphysics is vain. But that reality is not of a religious nature; it does not command belief, it is satisfied with "the willing suspension of disbelief." Just as pure science is wholly indifferent to religious issues, so is pure art. Paganism, heresy, even blasphemy may inspire great art, while some of the most orthodox hymns are perfectly vapid. Art and myth are one: neither constitutes an argument. Prometheus is not literally true because Aeschylus, Shelley, and Goethe wrote masterpieces about him.

CHAPTER XI

The authorities

I. THE CHURCH

Religion, to rise above the level of superstition, must be at the same time universal and definite. This balance is difficult to preserve: on one side yawns all-engulfing Pantheism; on the other stand multitudinous tribal creeds and rites. No thought can face Pantheism and live; tribalism is a more insidious peril. Seldom avowed by civilized men, it remains potent to-day.

There are two strains in Judaism, the universal and the tribal. They struggled through the whole Bible; they are still struggling for Israel's soul. The miraculous healing power of the French kings was a manifestation of tribalism; and so is the belief in the divine mission of Joan of Arc. There were obvious traces of tribalism under the Bismarckian empire: *Gott mit uns* was "our old German God." Nazism was an orgy of that primitive faith: "The German spirit is of God; the German spirit is God; and Hitler is its prophet." Tribalism is vigorous among the "Anglo-Saxons" on both sides of the Atlantic. Stephen Decatur's oft-applauded phrase: "My country, right or wrong!" can only mean: "Thou shalt have no other god beside America: not even God."

Religion is more than a code of ethics: morality depends upon the *mores* of a people, not upon its beliefs. It is also more than a myth: the Fighting God must have a name, a shape, and above all a history. For many earnest believers, Christianity is summed up in the great drama of Redemption: the Fall, the Cross, the Resurrection. But the dying god and the risen god were common themes in the "mystery" religions of the East. The depth and the beauty of the myth would not suffice to command belief: they would only elicit admiration. The myths created by Vigny in *Eloa* and by Hugo in *The End of Satan* appeal strongly to my imagination and my sentiments, but do not convince me in the least. A religion must be factually, historically true, or remain a fantastic poem. Jesus is not Tammuz, Attis or Mithra. Every "positive" religion, as distinct from the pale, abstract "natural" religion of the theists, must rest on historical evidence. There must be witnesses, and their testimony must be held valid. In the case of Christianity, these witnesses are the Church, the Bible, and the personality of Jesus.

By the Church, I mean first of all the Catholic Church; for it alone conceives of itself as a divinely appointed instrument for the preservation and the diffusion of the truth. It alone has a mystic existence: the others are merely societies formed among men. But I mean more than the Catholic Church: I mean the congregation of the faithful. The whole of Israel was in that sense the Church of God, the keeper of the Law: from Israel, the Catholic Church inherited the Old Testament. And, in a looser sense, the Church embraces all protestant sects as well: they are dissenting bodies, but within the general tradition. They too are collective preservers of an orthodoxy: they even claim to have restored to its purity the doctrine of the early, the original Church, that of the Apostles. They too are in possession of an historical truth.

I named the Church first, and not the Bible, as the foundation of the Christian faith. This should be evident. The Bible did not miraculously descend from Heaven at one time, complete with the instruments for deciphering and translating it, like the *Book of Mormon*. Both Testaments are the work of the Church. It was the "congregation" that selected the inspired books among the mass of those which advanced such a claim. Over some, there was some hesitancy. Others, revered and cherished by many, were accepted only as "deutero-canonical" or "apocryphal." Others still disappeared, for centuries or for ever: I have already alluded to the Book of Enoch, which was a power at the time of Christ. There is no criterion but the verdict of the Church;

there is no decisive internal evidence. Some of the books included in the canon lay no claim to divine inspiration. In some, words are spoken in the name of the Lord, or even placed in His mouth; but such passages are found also in apocryphal writings, and indeed in religious poetry through the ages. Medieval dramatists had God the Father speak in their own words; and so, centuries later, did Goethe, Victor Hugo, and Charles Péguy. All ministers who have seriously prepared themselves for their task know at least at second hand about the formation of the canon. They know therefore that the Church is the witness and warrant of the Bible. If the Church could err, and depart from the purity of the faith, it could err also in the selection of those documents upon which the faith is based.

If we are resolved to preserve the integrity of our thought, it becomes extraordinarily difficult to accept unquestioningly the divine claims of the Church. I am not embarrassed by the errors and crimes which are recorded in its annals. A divine institution must manifest itself to men and through men, in terms inevitably warped and soiled by the imperfection of human nature. The saints themselves have sinned, and even the Prince of the Apostles. No doubt there have been hypocrites and rogues among men whose office was holy: Dante, a reliable witness, met a Pope in hell. But the sins of mathematicians do not affect the truths of mathematics. A book like *Elmer Gantry*, even if every one of its assertions were supported by newspaper clippings, would prove nothing against religion.

More disconcerting is the fact that the congregation of the faithful is irremediably divided into three. The foundation remains the Hebrew Bible, which Christianity has never dared to discard. Yet those who knew the Bible best, those who had made it the core of their personal and collective life, rejected the new testament. Until the Jews accept Jesus as the fulfillment of prophecy, there will be the suspicion of a flaw in the title.

The schism between East and West, disastrous though it was, did not strike at the very root of the Church's claim. On the dogmatic plane, the differences were minor, and even the purely ecclesiastical conflicts could yet be composed in the spirit of

Christ. The Reformation was a deeper tragedy. Voices arose, accusing the Church of having erred for untold generations. Not only glaring abuses were denounced, but the discipline of fifteen hundred years. Apparently, the divine commission of the Church must have ceased when the canon was completed, as the powers of a constitutional assembly expire when its definite task is achieved. It might be held that thenceforth the Church became a Supreme Court, upholding, not creating, the Law. But the task of selecting the right interpretation among many possible meanings is as delicate and as essential as selecting the right book among many possible books. It is disturbing that God should have left us without guidance, and that the Church, still pretending to be the guardian of the faith, should turn out to be a blind leader of the blind.

The religion of the West has thus gone through two tremendous crises. First the Book was forcibly wrenched from the People of the Book; then it was wrenched again from the Church that had confirmed it, and had brought its second part into being. This second revolution took place without the direct divine intervention that sanctioned the first. No revelation, no miracles, justified Luther and Calvin when they split wide the body of ancient tradition. They took advantage of manifest abuses — and of many worldly ambitions as well — to sap the authority of the Church and substitute their own. Their own, not the gospel's. They knew that the interpretation of Holy Writ was no less essential than the letter, and they had no thought of leaving that interpretation to the vagaries of human reason. Calvin had a short way with dissenters; and although the articles of faith of modern churches are brief, the "party line" is very strictly drawn. It is not merely the letter that has been declared infallible, but the Protestant meaning attached to the letter. Romanists were long called idolators; the great humanitarians of a hundred years ago, who thought they had recaptured the spirit of Christ, but dissented from orthodox theologies, were branded as unbelievers.

The breach was not inevitable: a freer, richer, more generous spirit, accepting with joy the whole of the Renaissance, yet refusing to destroy the unity of the Christian world, was growing with such men as Erasmus and Rabelais. In France, Marguerite of Navarre united a free mind and a great love of art with deep and gentle piety; and her brother Francis I tried for years to ward off irremediable divisions. The most disastrous attitude in history is that of the *show-down.*

The Reformation made a mockery of *Catholicity*: that which, among Christians, had been believed by all men, at all times, and everywhere. It was demonstrated that the faith was not evident: doctors disagreed. Therefore it ceased to be unassailable. There is no hope of healing the breach. Those Catholics who start doubting the absolute claims of their church do not stop at the half-way house of Protestantism: a qualified certitude, a freedom dragging a heavy chain. It is inconceivable that Protestantism, in a body, should accept again the trammels that their ancestors found intolerable four hundred years ago. A church divided is a church self-condemned: Protestantism and Catholicism must unite before they can hope to win the world. But the path to unity is not a return to the past: the clashing sects can merge only by transcending themselves. And, if we strive for the Church Universal, it must embrace more than Catholicism and Protestantism. It must include all great faiths, and the faith that lives in honest doubt. For the dogmatist, this means suicide.

II. THE BOOK

Protestantism shifted the center of religion from the spirit of Christ preserved in the living Church to the spirit of Christ preserved in the living Book. The result, for certain sects at least, was a weakening of the specifically Christian element. The living Church began with Jesus: the authority of the Gospels is unique among sacred writings; for the Acts and the Epistles are merely corroborative, and many parts of the ancient Law have been abrogated. For the Bible-worshipper, on the contrary, the validity of the Old Testament remains unimpaired: not a jot or tittle of the Law has ceased to be binding. The Gospel is but the second part of Holy Writ. I have known ministers who felt perfectly at home in the stern, somber, and at times savage grandeur of the Old Testament, and ill at ease in the message of love which is the heart of the New. They can often be told by their predilection for the Hebrew term *Sabbath* instead of the Lord's Day. Their faith is first of all an offshoot of Judaism; they are heretical Jews in the same way as the Latter-Day Saints are heretical Christians. I have heard Presbyterian sermons and Methodist sermons inspired by religions which, under a single name, were poles asunder. It is true that I have heard the same minister preach a Presbyterian sermon in the morning, and a Methodist sermon at night: orthodoxy has no regard for the hobgoblin of little minds.

There were in the Renaissance two main currents which at times flowed irresistibly together, at times clashed and whirled in confusion. One was the revival of faith in the power and destiny of mankind: the Gargantuan appetite for learning, experience, creation, discovery, adventure, that made Ulrich von Hütten exclaim: "O century! It is a joy to be alive!" The other was the return to the thoughts, the ideals, but also the models, the patterns, the very texts of antiquity. Both tendencies are found in the Reformation as well. Like the Renaissance, the Reformation was a call to energy, an act of faith in *this* generation which dared to shake off the dread hand of custom, a cry of liberation: "At last, the calamitous night of the Goths is over!" Like the Renaissance, the Reformation was also the rediscovery, the recapture, of writings precious beyond price, now cleansed from the grime of ignorant centuries, and restored to their full freshness and vigor.

Humanism had assumed a double meaning: pride in the collective quest of mankind, Greek and Latin scholarship. The revived religious fervor likewise took a double form: the rejection of medieval shackles, scholastic subtleties, ecclesiastical complications, the teeming fetishism of superstitions; and also a return to a document which alone preserved the secret of life. The spirit needs the letter. The tragedy comes when the letter, anchored to the past, refuses to follow the free flight of the

spirit. Neo-classicism in art and literature was a retarding influence; but, in its full retrospective rigidity, it ruled only the
minds of a few pedants. The dynamic thinkers, Rabelais, Bacon,
Descartes, were forward looking. Shakespeare never was a slave
to the classic past. If Corneille accepted the rules of tragedy, it
was not because they came down from Aristotle, but because
they were in accord with *reason*. Boileau taught first of all that
we should love *reason*. Molière affirmed, with invincible common sense: "The ancients are the ancients, and we are the
people of today." The sacredness of the Greek and Latin clas-
sics could never become an absolute dogma: were it only because a consistent worshipper of the ancients would have had
to turn pagan. So the classical authorities were infallible —
within reason; the Bible was declared infallible *above reason*.
The bibliolatry of the scholars could never be as formidable an
obstacle to thought as the parallel bibliolatry of the theologians.

Protestantism asserts that the Bible stands by itself: it no
longer needs the Church, even if the Church, at one time, was
indispensable as "editor." But imagine the Bible presented today, as a book among other books, without the momentum of
centuries, without the added weight of other books by their
hundreds of thousands, without the backing of organizations
numbering hundreds of millions, the Bible stark and alone: do
you honestly believe that its unique, its infallible and sacred
character would be evident to critical minds? *The Bible is a tradition*, and Protestantism has shaken the force of tradition.

It is a problem whether a religion is stronger for finding expression in a book. The "mystery" religions which for a time
were the rivals of Christianity may have perished for lack of
scriptures. Perhaps the reverse is true: the scriptures disappeared
because the religions were defeated. Before the printing press,
the survival of books was precarious, and, in over a millennium
of exclusive domination, Christianity might well have eradicated
the last *written* traces of competing creeds. But in the days of
their greatest extension, rites, mysteries, secrets, initiation, were
mentioned, not sacred texts. The Prometheism of a hundred
years ago, linked with science, democracy, romanticism and

Utopian socialism, was, and I believe remains, a potent faith: but we find it hard to recognize it as such, because it lacks a scriptural canon. The possession of a Book is for Marxism a source of apparent strength, as it is for Mohammedanism.

On the other hand, I am told that the great religions of the East, although they possess sacred writings, have no final canon, no single, compendious, exclusive bible. The Book is obviously a peril as well as a force. For a unique and divinely inspired text must be infallible in the most literal sense. If we freely pick and choose — according to what criterion? — as Tolstoy ventured to do, the dogmatic authority of the Book disappears. So a biblical religion is caught between the twin curses of Liberalism, which is anarchy, and Literalism, which is death. So long as there were rival schools of Koranic interpretation, some historical, some boldly allegorical, the Koran lived. When Literalism, or Fundamentalism, triumphed, the Koran became a tomb; and Arabic civilization, at one time the most active in the world, has not been able to lift that stone.

I gladly admit that the Bible, if it were discovered today, would take its place among the masterpieces of mankind. I was brought up on Pascal, Vigny, Hugo, and Renan, who owed far more to the Bible than to classical antiquity. Longinus was perhaps the first to recognize, in aesthetic terms, the *sublimity* of the Hebrew scriptures. But *Credo quia pulchrum*, so freely used by Chateaubriand and James Branch Cabell, is a dangerously double-edged argument. For the puritans of all faiths, beauty is a snare, not a proof: true believers are not so easy to persuade as the judges of Phryne. To pass on the merits of God's writings verges on sacrilege, as it would be to dwell on the "good looks" of the Virgin Mary.[1]

If by the the standard of literary excellence, the Book of Job ranks at least on a level with *Prometheus Bound* or *Faust*; if Ecclesiastes delves far deeper than La Rochefoucauld, Schopen-

[1] I remember a snatch from a hymn I used to sing in my childhood:
"Je vous salue, auguste et sainte Reine,
Dont la beauté ravit les immortels . . ."
I do not remember whether I was edified at the time; today the words have a baroque nostalgic appeal.

hauer, or Hemingway; if the Book of Jonah vies with the best philosophical tales of Voltaire; if every epithalamion in profane literature is tepid compared with the ardent sensuality of the Song of Solomon, if the weirdest visions of our surrealists seem tame by the side of the Apocalypse; if above all the Psalms and the great prophets reach the heights and depths of religious lyric poetry; on the other hand the historical parts of the Bible seem stiff and primitive to readers of Thucydides, Livy, Tacitus; and the ritual codes afford but the most unpalatable fare. Suppose that, on an artistic basis, we were to compile a Bible of Mankind: Lucretius, Dante, Milton, Shelley, and even Lamennais and Nietzsche would have better claims than James or Jude or even Obadiah.

Matthew Arnold pleaded cogently that the Bible be read and understood as literature. But this implies giving up all claims to factual infallibility. The opening and the closing books, Genesis and Revelation, are as impressive as anything ever conceived by man. But impressiveness is no test of truth. Don Quixote is more impressive than Cervantes, Hamlet than Shakespeare, Satan than Milton, Faust than Goethe. But on the down-to-earth level of material facts, the authors did exist in the flesh, the poetic characters are figments. It is perfectly true that I prize those figments far above most of my fellow-men; but I am compelled to recognize an essential difference. Now I am willing to stand for the spiritual veracity of the Bible against the materialists. Those who insist that some marine monster did swallow, then evict, the prophet Jonah are in my opinion guilty of a gross breach of taste. The Book of Jonah begins like a splendid yarn, better than *Sinbad the Sailor*; it continues with a psalm not unworthy of King David; it ends with a lesson in humility, gentleness, and humor most desperately needed in our days of wrath. But there is little sense in affirming that it is literally true.

Lyell was denounced as an enemy of religion, because he doubted the accepted date of creation, which Bishop Ussher had worked out to a day. "Not the age of rocks, but the Rock of Ages" should be the guide of our thought. Today His Holiness

himself has added a few billion years to the past of our planet.
But then the scientific validity of the Bible is destroyed. What
shall we say? That some parts of the Book are factually true,
and others allegorical? That the scribes, fallible men, mixed the
errors of their time with the divine truth? That God Himself
tempered His revelation to the primitive minds of His chosen
prophets? That God's truth, like God Himself, cannot be contem-
plated face to face? In every case, if you deviate by one iota from
the strictest literalism, you must admit that the Bible as we have
it is compounded of verities and errors. And again, what re-
agent will enable us to separate the pure gold from the dross?
The laws of historical evidence? The laws of reason? The moral
sense of a Rousseau or a Kant? In one way or another, we de-
throne revelation as the sole basis of our faith.

If we face the fundamental problem without flinching, the
details of Biblical criticism become almost irrelevant. It is not
necessary to be a profound Hebrew scholar to recognize that
there are in Genesis several traditions which were imperfectly
fused. Woman was created twice over: there is a vast literature
— including such theological authorities as Anatole France and
John Erskine — about Adam's first wife, Lilith.[2] The orthodox
assure themselves that there must be some way of reconciling
the conflicting genealogies of Joseph (which, if the Virgin Birth
is admitted, are not the genealogies of Christ). But this implies
that there must have been at some point a confusion of names
or persons, which again saps the fundamental dogma of literal
inspiration. It is easy to say that the objections of Bayle and
Voltaire are antiquated, shallow, flippant; and I have no doubt
that there are in the most conservative seminaries biblical scholars more learned than Voltaire and Bayle. Still, the rudimentary
Questions of Zapata have not been answered to this day. Until
they are, we must consider the Bible as a splendid and perplex-
ing aggregate of inspired visions, righteous anger, disenchanted

---

[2] In Talmudic tradition, Lilith became a creature of evil, a ghoul.
I came across a heresy which has at least weird logic in its favor. Lilith,
who did not fall with Adam, did not know death; neither did she come
under the curse of the original sin. *Ergo*: she is the Immaculate Conception.

wisdom, folklore, ritual, and most unedifying chronicles. Bibliolatry cannot serve as the foundation for a universal faith.

III. THE SAVIOUR

Protestantism sacrificed the Church and preserved the Book. Innumerable believers, openly or secretly, sacrifice the Book and preserve the Saviour. This is not true of our confused age only. The mystics have constantly sought and attained the direct experience of Christ. Others, on an earthly plane, attempt to reach the essence of His person and of His message, through the blurred tradition, the imperfect record, the fallible witnesses. Spiritual truth cannot be revealed suddenly in its blinding splendor: it is meet that we should see as through a glass, darkly. We have to conquer truth, and deserve truth, through our own efforts. That is why Christians are still seeking Christ, beyond the Church, and beyond the Book.

Some thirty years ago, an accident — the centennial of Napoleon's death — induced me to reflect on the Napoleonic Legend. My purpose was not "debunking." By legend, I did not mean a pack of lies. I wanted to understand a phenomenon far transcending, in space and time, Napoleon's earthly career: for it kept growing after his downfall and his death, and it is alive to-day. Legend, as I understand it, is the emotional response which magnifies, transforms, transmutes actual events. There are legends, like that of Washington, in which the shimmering aura simply emphasizes the sharp outline of the historical figure. There are legends, like that of Lincoln, in which, while the plain facts are not distorted, imagination and sentiment blur the line that separates reality from myth and symbol. There are legends in which the man and the epic character are both vivid, but different: the Charlemagne of the eighth century bears only a distant likeness to the Charlemagne of the eleventh. There are legends in which the material substratum is attenuated to the vanishing point: we are not quite sure that King Arthur ever lived; we are almost certain that William Tell never did.

History is more than mere chronicle; and, in the great epic

drama that it offers us, the protagonists are more than men: they are ideas revealed through events, and events magnified into myths. The individual hero ceases to be merely an ailing, fallible, bewildered man: he stands for a cause, were it only for a passion. And by a similar but reversed process, abstractions become personified. The nations are thought of as alive: André Siegfried — an unexpected epigone of German Romanticism — teaches us that they have souls. Institutions like the Republic or the Monarchy, and movements too, are endowed with a mind, a purpose, an individuality. For a hundred years, the Revolution was to many Frenchmen a goddess, beneficent and terrible; to others, a hag spewed from hell.

The most objective historians, just because they spurn imagination and sentiment, "ignore" the legend, which is another way of taking it for granted. They ascertain the details: they are too "realistic" to investigate the myths which give the details their significance. Thus Kircheisen, a plodding conscientious scholar, accumulated facts about Napoleon, facts which were used to make the Legend more vivid; but he never paused to consider the nature and the validity of the Legend itself. So he could tell you that every man in the Empire and its satellites was eager to die for the hero, and, on the same page, quote a letter from Napoleon to the Prefect of the Aube Department, ordering him to round up draft-evaders. The bulk of Napoleonic scholarship seeks accuracy in details, but never challenges the orthodox conception: the superhuman stature of the titan.

I could not fail to be impressed with the resemblance between the legend of Napoleon and that of Christ. The men who wrote the saga, and Napoleon himself, deliberately emphasized the common elements. Pérès[3] and Whately[4] in their clever little books purporting to demonstrate that Napoleon never existed, had in mind the mythicists (oddly enough, Napoleon was among them) who doubted that Jesus had ever trod this earth. Napoleon as the Messiah of Democracy was a commonplace in the thirties

[3] Jean-Baptiste Pérès, *Comme quoi Napoléon n'a jamais existé*, 1817.
[4] Richard Whately, later Archbishop of Dublin, *Historic Doubts Relative to Napoleon Buonaparte*, 1819.

and forties. Dreams of a second coming were rife, influenced perhaps by the Barbarossa legend. For many, the Second Empire was an *Ersatz* for that dream. In that age of splendid confusion, Napoleon, Jesus, Prometheus, Don Juan, Faust, and the Wandering Jew were all haunting the fervid imagination of men. But the mystic and messianic conception of Napoleon survived Romanticism, and lingered through the realistic age. For Léon Bloy and Dmitri Merezhkovsky, Napoleon was not purely of this earth. If a canny Scottish doctor, Robert McNair Wilson, entitled his book *Napoleon: The Man*, he meant something deeper than a study in personality; for him as for the Romanticists, Napoleon was *l'Homme*, The Man par excellence, the apex and symbol of all humanity, the Son of Man.

There always was in my mind a difference between the Napoleonic Legend and the Christ Legend. I studied Napoleon, not to attack, but to understand. But I realized increasingly that his myth was evil. I did my best to curb my hostility: I could not deny its presence. Napoleon stands for material success, contempt for man, deceit, and above all, force. There are in his fame elements of brutality, and worse, of vulgarity, which are abhorrent to me. Napoleon is the supreme "realist," the great parvenu, the gang leader *in excelsis*, the idol of robber barons. He has but one redeeming feature: a touch of insanity. For the Jesus legend, on the contrary, I never felt anything but sympathy and reverence. I never sought to expose or destroy it; my only desire was to probe and assimilate its significance, to the utmost of my ability. If I strayed from conventional paths, it was in the assurance that God does not need our lies, and that the freer our faith is from delusions, the more effective it will prove.

In attempting to order my thoughts, I find at least eight different conceptions of Christ, and they fail to make a convincing composite picture. Three of them were presented to me when I was still in the grades. The first was orthodoxy, for I dutifully learned my catechism. The second was the free Christianity of the later Hugo: in my family, Victor Hugo was a prophet, and I thumbed illustrated copies of his works before I was able to

read. The third was Renan's purely historical approach: his
Life of Jesus was among our slender store of books.⁵ In comparison, the other five are shades or subdivisions of secondary
importance. The dogmatic, the mystic-mythical, and the historical are fundamental.

In the literal sense of the word, Renan's *Life of Jesus* enchanted me. It gave me delight, and seemed magically to resolve
all discords. I found it beautiful and tender, the very reverse of
Voltaire's corrosive irony. It did not dispel the fragrance of incense that I brought back from Sainte Clotilde's. Yet I could feel
also that it was scholarly, free from the timidities and prejudices
which are too often associated with piety. It required no capitulation of that scientific conscience which my lay teachers were
striving to foster. Parts of it seemed to me even then too idyllic:
I understood how their sweetness would cloy, for those who
cannot avert their eyes for a moment from the tragic mystery of
the Cross. But the Passion was a matter of a few hours, the
arraignment, betrayal, and judgment, of a few days; and the
mission of Christ lasted three years. The gentle, happy side of
Jesus's life and teaching cannot be ignored. He wanted us to be,
not fierce angry men like John Calvin and Jonathan Edwards,
but little children. It is unjust to say that Renan "concocted
candies with a flavor of the infinite." He was not mawkish: he
was serene. He appears soft only because he refused to be rough.
Good judges of French literature know that both his style and
his thought were firm. Under their smooth finish, they had an
armature of well-tempered steel.

The other volumes of Renan's great work, *The Origins of
Christianity*, led me beyond his *Life of Jesus* and made me
realize the ultimate failure, *as history*, of his most famous book.
It was good that a biography of Jesus be attempted, strictly according to the canons of historical science; and Renan was admirably qualified to make the attempt. He knew orthodoxy from
within: his childhood and youth had been profoundly devout;

⁵ I have already treated at some length of Renan, and particularly of
his *Life of Jesus* in my *French Prophets of Yesterday* (1913) and *Personal Equation* (1948). My point of view has not radically changed.
Repetition is inevitable, and is acknowledged without apology.

and to his dying day he remained a priest at heart. He was a scholar, and took just pride in his *Corpus Inscriptionum Semiticarum*. And he had the artistic virtues which are indispensable to the great historian: lucidity and a sense of composition first of all, but, far above these, insight, sympathy, a deep and tranquil understanding of life. He knew at first hand, and used with marvelous effect the "Fifth Gospel," the landscape of Judaea, and the immemorial existence of its inhabitants, unaltered since Jesus was a child. With all these gifts, he ventured to give us the positivistic biography of an "incomparable man." As history, the book, with all its scientific apparatus, brings no certainty; as a psychological hypothesis, as the reconstruction of a living mind, it brings no conviction.

I feel certain that no one could succeed where Renan has failed, because the failure is inherent in the very nature of the effort. The place of the *man* Jesus in factual history is infinitesimal; or rather it is a mere shadow. We have no contemporary evidence from outside sources. The earliest Christian documents that have survived are the Epistles of Paul, who had not seen Jesus in the flesh; and they give no coherent account of his earthly career. The Gospels were compiled after the actual witnesses had passed away: why should the disciples write a record, when they thought the end of the world was at hand? To deny the miracles off-hand would be question-begging; but there are discrepancies of all kinds in the sacred narratives which seriously impair the validity of the testimonies. When we see how soon and how radically news can be distorted even in our "scientific age," we wonder what confidence can be placed in oral tradition, nearly two thousand years ago, among simple unlettered folk in the superstitious East. The sole scientific verdict, free from religious bias, would be the one found in Anatole France's *Procurator of Judaea*: like Pilate, history has forgotten.

So slender is the evidence for the historical Jesus that his earthly existence has been denied altogether. There was in the Enlightenment a strain of extreme rationalism, an inclination to reject every belief that was not within the range of common sense. All "positive" (i.e., historical) religions stood condemned as superstitions. At the origin of every one stood primitive gullibility, worked upon by deliberate fraud, as in the case of Mohammed.[6] The lives of all religious founders were filled with miracles, therefore they could not be true. Fontenelle led the way by challenging — what could be safer? — the miracles of *pagan* antiquity. But if the great minds of the classic past had thus been deluded, can we be sure of our own immunity? The road was cleared for Bayle, Voltaire, and Hume.

The common run of eighteenth-century doubters were shallow enough; but so were the common run of eighteenth-century believers. The skeptical attitude is not to be dismissed as mere rococo flippancy. We must remember that there had been early Christian heretics denying the human, that is to say the historical, character of Jesus, in order to make Him all divine. We must remember also that it was skepticism that made the comparative study of religions possible: without it, there was room only for apologetics. Dupuis, with his *Origins of All Cults,* was a forerunner of Sir James Frazer. And finally, we should bear in mind that *myth* is not of necessity a derogatory term: Vico had already taught that myths could be the embodiment of deep collective experiences, memories, and aspirations. So doubts about the historical character of Jesus were not simply chance weapons in the anticlerical crusade. We have already alluded to the fact that Napoleon was aware of the idea, and considered it without disfavor. Napoleon was too genuine a "realist" to be a Christian at heart. If he professed to be a member of the Church, and indeed its temporal head, it was without any deep-lying faith in its divine mission. He spoke in the same tone of "my gendarmes, my prefects, my bishops."

Romanticism, as we have seen, was haunted with gigantic ghosts: Christ Himself one in that teeming Pantheon. By totally different methods, rationalism and romanticism were both sapping the historicity of Jesus. Scholarship followed, *pede claudo.* Early in his manifold career, Albert Schweitzer wrote a learned

---

[6] This attitude was not created by the Voltairians; in the middle ages, as early as the days of Frederick II, *Stupor Mundi,* there had been persistent whispers about *The Book of the Three Impostors,* i.e., Moses, Jesus, and Mohammed.

book: *The Quest of the Historical Jesus: A Critical Study of Its Progress from Reimarus to Wrede*; and nearly half a century later, after a vast circuit of thought, he was more inclined than ever to minimize the man Jesus, the purely historical figure that Renan had attempted to portray. Perhaps the boldest and most ingenious work in that line is that of Arthur Drews: we know that there was a god Jesus; we have no convincing trace of a man Jesus. Georg Brandes and Paul Couchoud popularized this theory; and Guignebert, once a leader of the Modernists, and a reputable historian, when he attempted to refute Couchoud, came to the same guarded conclusion as Schweitzer: there probably was a man Jesus; but what we know about him is negligible. *And, to a truly religious mind, the problem is of minor importance.*

Ingenuous believers shudder at the thought that Christ was perhaps not a creature of flesh and blood, as they had been taught; that he lived in the same shadowy realm as Osiris, or Tammuz, or Santa Claus. Paradoxically, the Mythicists are closer to Christian orthodoxy than the Historicists. The consternation of simple souls would be still greater, if Christ were shown to be *mere* man: a St. Francis of Assisi with a dash of Savonarola. They will not admit that He *became* divine, as did the Roman emperors. He is not a promoted man, but an incarnate god. The center of orthodox faith is the Eternal Christ, Who existed before the man Jesus.

If the gospel were to lose its validity as a chronicle of earthly events, it might acquire even greater significance as an allegory or symbol. Faith need not be diminished by being purified. A third Reformation would be needed. The first, Protestantism, destroyed the absolute authority of the Church. The second — the Higher Criticism — questioned the literal inerrancy of the Book. The third might discard, as no longer needed, what vestiges remain of the historical basis. To borrow the words of Joachim a Floris, this would be the gospel no longer fastened to a date in time, the *Gospel Everlasting.*

I have been by profession a student of literature all my life, and my own guide in this case has been literary criticism. I cannot accept in its entirety the mythical theory, because the figure of Jesus in the gospel is alive, whereas Attis or Mithra are not. (Again, I am hopelessly in the dark: perhaps Mithra *was* alive in the souls of his believers.) Poets create life: it is a truism that Don Quixote is more alive than Cervantes, and George F. Babbitt than Sinclair Lewis. It is the motives of Hamlet, not of Shakespeare, that we are probing; and people flock eagerly to see the cell from which Dantès escaped to become Monte Cristo. To innumerable readers Bishop Myriel and Jean Valjean are alive. We might find at the origin of Christianity, not a Man who inspired a Book, but a Book that gave life to a Man.

Now, the internal *literary* evidence is against such an interpretation. For the character and the sayings of Jesus are so convincing that only a master could have conceived them. Only a genius could have invented the great cry: *Eloi, Eloi, lama sabachthani?* The compilers of the Gospels, at least of the three Synoptics, were no such masters. Their subject is obviously beyond them; they report as faithfully as they can, but with lapses that reveal their limitations. When Christ is not speaking, the tone of the narrative is commonplace.

It is not absolutely inconceivable that an unknown poet may have started "The Song of Jesus," without leaving any authentic text. Who knows? He may have been illiterate, versed only in scriptural lore. Garbled versions, each carrying some reflection of the original light, may have proliferated, at a time when copyright laws were not strictly enforced. Of these versions, four were finally adopted as canonical: something akin to the emergence of the Homeric poems, according to the folklorists. But, in the case of Homer and in the case of the Gospels, this hypothesis, wholly unproved, strains belief. So far as I am concerned, it strains it beyond the breaking point.

So, with no great assurance, I am inclined to admit that there was a man Jesus, who said most of the things ascribed to him in the Gospels. Even the contradictions add to the verisimilitude: for only the automata fabricated by second-rate writers possess the deadly gift of consistency. But our knowledge is far too slender and too uncertain to justify a definite biography of the

Renanian type. This Master, dimly surmised, found response, because there was readiness. He did not preach in a wilderness without echoes. In this sense, Christianity preceded Christ, demanded Christ, in the same way that Rousseauism, floating in the public mind, was waiting for Rousseau to give it a name. He found response because he brought the message that many had been expecting; but above all because he had the virtue of a poet. He expressed and revealed himself while voicing the aspirations of mankind. He crystallized a preëxisting ideal, but he colored it with his own personality. And undoubtedly, whatever claims he may have advanced for himself, he was raised by his followers from the purely human plane to the symbolical, which we may call either mythical or divine.

We have so far three conceptions of Christ: the man Jesus of Renan, the god Jesus of Drews, the Jesus of poetry and art, author or subject of "the greatest story ever told." In the fourth place comes Jesus the moral teacher. It matters not whether he be man, god, or the hero of an edifying romance. We may forget, we may choose to ignore, who it was that put up the road sign, who discovered the scientific law: the problem is whether the sign is right, whether the law is true. This conception was, in the main, that of Tolstoy. He drew the moral essence from the gospel; that became his norm, and he felt free to recast the Gospels according to his moral criterion. Whatever was in accord with the Christian spirit must be authentic; whatever contradicted it was a distortion or an interpolation. Tolstoy believed himself a follower of Christ; so did Victor Hugo and Dostoevsky. Gandhi did not: he was a fellow-traveler. Christ was to be revered, so long as he and Gandhi were in agreement; but Christ was not the source of Gandhi's inspiration.

The moral message of Christ is profound and paradoxical. It is not absolutely unique, even in the West: there are traces of meekness, humility, *misericordia*, in the prophets and psalmists of Israel; and in the lucid, severe, unsentimental tradition of Greco-Roman thought. But they are only gleams. Most religions are based on pride: stoic pride, pride of race or nation, the fierce pride of the fighter. It is the miracle of history that Christianity could insert itself into the haughty framework of the Roman world; maintain itself among the Barbarians, drunk with brutal pride; be acknowledged by the feudal barons, whose ideal was prowess and whose trade was fighting; that it should force itself upon Elizabeth and Louis XIV, pride incarnate, personal pride, national pride; that it should receive lip-service even today, when our gods are so manifestly wealth and power. Nietzsche is our prophet, but we disown him. Christ is the pattern of the "do-gooders" we despise, yet he is our God.

This gives the clue to the paradox: Christ is not our moral leader, for the very reason that he is divine. We interpret his words: "My kingdom is not of this world," as meaning: "This world is not Christ's kingdom; his writ does not run here below; therefore we must be *realistic.*" Man is no angel: whoso attempts to play the angel plays the fool. In spite of Thomas a Kempis, we cannot *imitate* our Lord: His nature is too different from ours.[7]

There is a point at which meekness itself turns to righteous anger. Beside the gentle Jesus stands the rebel who denounced evil-doers and called woe upon them. That Jesus takes his place in the tradition of the prophets, those men of holy wrath who dared to attack the rich, the priests and the kings. We cannot forget that Christ scourged the money changers out of the Temple, and that he came to bring not peace but a sword. I remember an Arab agitator I heard in Algiers in 1937. There was no meekness about him: the French might have called him a subversive and a rabble-rouser. But there was something "sacred," that is to say mysterious and awe-inspiring, about the flame of his fanaticism. If Jesus was a man, those two contrasting aspects of his message were not incompatible: love of the oppressed easily turns into hatred of the oppressor. Sacrilegious as it may sound,

---

[7] This is excellently illustrated in a familiar parable. A young lady who, at some religious meeting, had been given a seat next to a Negro, rushed from the hall in indignation. She was rebuked: "Do you think this is the way Jesus would have behaved?" — "Ah! But Jesus came from Heaven; I come from Alabama, and I won't stand it." Premier Daniel François Malan, of South Africa, does not dare to put his case with such engaging frankness.

even Hitler could claim that he was moved by love: love for the
German people, robbed, shackled, offended, and despised. This
yielding to anger was perhaps the inner flaw that made Jesus so
human and so tragic. The agitator, the rebel in him had to
acknowledge and welcome defeat, which was his purification.

Radically different from the moral aspect of Jesus is the
metaphysical. It is, I believe, as plainly Greek as the "mythical"
is Asiatic. The Gospel of St. John, its noblest expression, is Neo-
Platonic. We are in a world of eternal ideas: "In the beginning
was the Word, and the Word was with God, and the Word was
God." It is a marvelous indistinct vision, dark with excess of
light; and for twenty centuries, logicians have attempted to
reduce this glory to a neat rational scheme. To me this effort
seems like holding a wire mesh before the sun, and exulting:
"Behold, I have the secret of the sun!" Through these twenty
centuries, theologians have been disputing, most acrimoniously,
about the merits of their litle wire patterns. I do not believe that
the world at large ever was deeply interested. If people fought
and tortured in the name of some theological point, it was because of their fighting instinct: *filioque*, or Arianism, or tran-
substantiation, offered as good a pretext as any. I know that the
latest Father of the Church, Mortimer Adler, is a supremely
intelligent man. I am ready to praise the delicacy, the intricacy,
the fearful symmetry of his wire mesh, which he inherited from
the greatest master of the craft, St. Thomas Aquinas. But the
world does not need that elaborate screen.

Our reason balks at the thought that so many great men, for
so many generations, should have labored so diligently and so
utterly in vain. But Nature is a spendthrift, and history is full
of misspent energies. The Christians do not believe that the
theologians of other faiths are seriously contributing to the truth.
As a religion, Paganism was sheer waste. It cannot even be
credited with the marvelous achievements of Greek art: the
chronique scandaleuse of Olympus was not necessary to produce
the Venus of Milo. From the dawn of time, men have fought.
They have shown admirable courage, endurance, ingenuity, and,

in recent ages, an incredible command of elaborate techniques. And yet the wise have always known that fighting was folly. I admire St. Thomas and I admire Napoleon: again, I feel very humble before them. But to admire is not to endorse.

The point that Schweitzer most emphasizes in his interpretation of Jesus is the eschatological. Eschatology differs from metaphysics: it is a prophetic doctrine, not an interpretation of eternal law. It forecasts "the last things," the divine completion of world history. Its chief features are the Second Coming, the end of this earthly dispensation, the Millennium, and the Last Judgment. Schweitzer argues convincingly that this was the essence of Christ's message: it was the threat and the promise that filled the minds of his immediate disciples. Both Schweitzer and Niebuhr, who are reverent but fearless, admit that Christ was mistaken. The first generation lived in false hopes. The hopes were deferred, century after century. For many Christians, they have receded to a dim secondary place in their faith. But even in our sober days, many souls, not all of them professed Christians, are still haunted with apocalyptic dreams.

It might be said that Jesus was in error only about the timing of his prophecies; or even that his disciples, in the eagerness of their own desire, wrongly interpreted his dark sayings. The nature of prophecy is to be cryptic: sybils and oracles spoke in riddles. It is natural that people should anticipate Armageddon and the Millennium within their lifetime. In their thought, they are more "subversive" than any revolutionary party. It is not merely a political regime which they hope to see tumble down, but the whole physical universe, so that there will be a new heaven and a new earth.

If we brush aside the timetable with which the early Christians deluded themselves, Christ's eschatology still appeals to us with singular power. The coming of the Kingdom may be interpreted as a "myth" in the sense that Georges Sorel gave to the word: an ideal which guides our thought and action, which is constantly in process of realization in our hearts and in our lives, and yet which is not capable of absolute fulfillment. The kingdom is here, and the kingdom will never come. Our effort is the asymptote of that ideal: the two will meet only when time is no more.

So the Christ conceived by Schweitzer, in his last meditations, is not a man who lived nineteen centuries ago, nor an eternal static Logos, but the spiritual life force, the "vital urge" of creative evolution, an "increasing purpose," the end of which is beyond our bournes of time and space. That purpose is of God; that purpose is God; yet its only manifestation on earth is the consciousness and conscience of humanity. Schweitzer, like Tennyson, hails "the Christ that is to be," when the Son of Man and the Son of God become at last one person.

This conception can be reconciled with the tradition, if the tradition ceases to be static, acquires momentum, is willing to increase from precedent to precedent. If we seek the kingdom *within* ourselves, by communing with the Christ spirit in us, we shall also inevitably build it *among* ourselves. Again, we are drawing very close to the great faith of the Romantic age, the Prometheism or Neo-Christianity of Shelley, Saint-Simon, Lamennais, Hugo. But we must admit that such a conception cannot be turned into a dogma. Like the Fighting God, it is an *as if*, an allegory; deeper than an allegory, it is a symbol, the adumbration of things which human eyes can never see, nor human tongues utter. Perhaps, for the mystics, the veil between symbol and reality vanishes like a morning mist. But the only language of the mystic is silence.

CHAPTER XII

Christianity and free thought

I am writing this testament without defiance and without fear: at this hour, why should I pretend, to man or to God? I have no desire to placate and no desire to offend. I hate violent disruption, material or spiritual. I should like to call myself a Christian. I am bound to explain why I do not feel at liberty to do so.

I have preserved the most respectful and affectionate memories of my teachers at Sainte Clotilde's. The man whose friendship I prize above all others is a priest. My daughter is a grateful child of the Sacred Heart. If in politics I am a determined anticlerical, it is not through any hostility to religion or to the clergy. I profess against the deadly "realistic" heresy of our time that the spirit of religion and the spirit of government should be the same. But I do not want any particular class of men to dominate the state. Not the proletarians, and not the capitalists; not the lawyers, and not the military; not the scientists, and not the clergy; and above all, not the politicians.

If I am steeped in the Catholic tradition, I know Protestantism from within. My four brothers-in-law, as dear as if they were brothers in blood, had long honored careers in the Presbyterian ministry. In England and America, it is with Protestants that I most naturally associated. I may add that from the days of the Dreyfus crisis I have always felt the greatest sympathy for the Jews. In a severe illness, the visits, I might say the ministration, of Rabbi Goldenson brought me great comfort. My three years at Brandeis University (1950–1953) were a very pleasant experience, the long Indian summer of my academic life. It was a privilege to be identified more closely with one of the most ancient and most profound traditions of mankind. Familiarity, far from lessening respect, deepened it into affection. This experience made me realize the incredible variety of Jewish types: *the* Jew, like *the* American, is the merest abstraction. It also brought home to me the fact that the noblest part of a tradition is found in aspiration rather than in fulfillment. No tradition can be true to its inner law unless it transcends itself. The ideal Jew is the Jew that is to be; and he will no longer be a Jew, but Man, and the Son of Man.

It was not inevitable, but it was natural enough, that I should join the Episcopal Church, in which the spirit and the traditions of Catholicism are so miraculously blended. It is a sign of this harmony that the church today should be able to erect such masterpieces of *living* Gothic — not antiquarian pastiches — as St. John the Divine and the Liverpool Cathedral. The Anglican compromise is English to the marrow, not universal: but England had become, and remained for ten crucial years, my second intellectual home. My mother had joined a curious little congregation, the Gallican Church, obstinately attached to the strictest Catholic doctrine and persuaded that in the last two centuries Rome had strayed from the appointed path. It offered at least a shadow of that Gallicanism which for six hundred years had placed such a commanding part in the ecclesiastical history of France. Anglicanism and Gallicanism, if not twins, are at least cousins, and it was easy for me to pass from the one to the other.

I was not deterred by the irony which freethinkers, rigid dogmatists, and popular revivalists alike would pour on the Establishment. I was duly warned that, according to Oxford, "there is no God, and Jesus Christ is His son." I was told I would have to choose between the Latitudinarians, the Platitudinarians, and the Attitudinarians. In America, I was constantly assailed with the story of the mammy who, as she filled the sacred edifice with pious ejaculations, was sternly rebuked: "Why, Mammy! Don't you know that the Episcopal Church is no place to get religion?" I smiled, and shrugged, and went my way. My one misgiving was that the church was too gentlemanly a club for a man who, by birth and conviction, belonged to the people. At any rate, I have never presumed, and I have never been snubbed. It may be that I took my Anglican membership in the same spirit as my commission in the American army: a great honor, with a delightful undertone of paradox. Be this as it may, an English church at dusk — not merely Canterbury or Durham, but the humblest parish — is the place where I feel most perfectly at peace. If my bishop would permit, I still should like to call myself an Episcopalian: an agnostic absentee Episcopalian.

Yet I am aware that all this is sentiment, aestheticism, the love of the dim religious light and the pealing organ, the inveterate Toryism of the professional historian. I hold with Pascal that the whole dignity of man lies in his thought; and even, with Descartes, that the very existence of man depends upon his thought. No thought is worthy of the name, unless it be free; and no church, not even the Episcopal, not even the Unitarian, will unreservedly acknowledge the primacy of free thought. Of course, it would be easy to equivocate. My faith in the Fighting God and in the building of the Kingdom could easily be expressed in terms that would not shock the most scrupulous conservatives. But I repeat that I do not accept these great metaphors as dogmas. I have known "liberal" Protestants who balked at the Resurrection, but spoke with unction of "Christ's victory over death," hoping that the orthodox, simple souls, would not see the catch. With the liberalism that is looseness and rests upon ambiguity, I have nothing whatever to do.

Honesty compels me to go a long step farther. Among the educated at any rate, natural religion is quite respectable. I have no claim even to that last shred of respectability. I cannot call myself a theist or a deist. No one prevents me, of course, from defining God as "the mystery that makes for righteousness." But Theism will not be satisfied with mystery. It insists on using terms which have an actual content: Being, Spirit, Person, Power, Creator, Ruler. Every one of these words contains at least the implication of a dogma. I repeat that I have no faith in the Metaphysical God, the Absolute: so far as human

thought is concerned, *All* and *Nothing* are one. The Uncreated
Creator seems to me an instance of the Elephant-and-Tortoise
fallacy: the problem is shifted, not solved. I cannot be satisfied with the argument of Voltaire and Rousseau, renewed quite
recently by my respected friend Dr. Monroe Deutsch: the
marvelous mechanism of this world demands a supreme artificer. Material nature seems to me full of imperfections: catastrophes, death, disease, waste, the relentless struggle for survival: it is we who are attempting to establish a certain measure
of order and fairness in that soulless chaos. One thing alone
bears out the time-honored comparison of this world with a
clock: the course of the heavenly bodies, so regular that eclipses
can be foretold. But this applies only to a mechanical universe,
without a sense of liberty, and therefore of moral value: the
God of Cybernetics does not fire my soul. And even the chrono-
metric regularity of the cosmos is open to question. Our solar
system itself is the result of some remote cataclysm, and may
be heading toward some kind of disruption. The millennia of
faultless regularity between these apocalypses are flashes in the
perspective of infinite time, and nonexistent *sub specie aeterni-
tatis.* When it comes to the starry heavens, wisdom spoke
through the lips of the great mathematician Laplace: we have
no need for the theistic hypothesis.

   Yes, the God of Voltaire, the God that "we should invent if
he did not exist," prolongs into the unknown the realm of
purely human experience and purely human reason, but cannot take us beyond. He is simply a magnified man. He fits in
admirably with an even better known epigram of the Patriarch:
"If God made man in His own image, man returned the
compliment." Atheism, a vacuum, is not the core of my
thought. I am not interested in it: I have no need for that
purely negative hypothesis. But I have the right to reject, as
unnecessary, illogical, and idolatrous, the anthropomorphic
doctrine. I know that in all denominations there are many who
are not mere conformists, and who have what I consider as
the essential religious experience: the sense of mystery and the
desire to do good. They pour life into their symbols: they do

not receive life from these symbols. But they refuse to consider their creeds as symbolic. They insist upon subordinating the life-giving experience to formal assertions which to me are superstitious or irrelevant.

This is my deepest objection to all the creeds: *their inveterate, their irremediable materialism.* The Sacred Books contain far more than ethical commands and visions of the spiritual world: they are also records, in the fields of astronomy, geology, geography, and history, and those records purport to be the inspired word of God. Literalism cannot be expunged without destroying the supernatural claims of the churches. I know that the Pope has receded from the position that Genesis was sound "natural science," without jeopardizing his own infallibility; but humble mortals do not possess this miraculous gift of facing both ways. The Bible must be different from folklore, epic poetry, myth. The Gospels, in particular, leave no room for equivocation. It was not purely the spirit of Christ that, after his death, filled the hearts of his disciples: it was his body of flesh and blood that appeared before their eyes, and the fingers of St. Thomas probed his wounds. It was that earthly body, not a dissolving vision, that ascended into heaven to sit at the right hand of God. It is our own bones and tissues that will be reconstituted (with all the infirmities and ailments that burdened us?) and live for ever at the foot of the great white throne. I can only repeat that these "realistic" stories only desecrate the hereafter, rob the mystery of its awe and splendor. The fight of religious free thought against orthodoxy is the fight of spiritual truth against material pseudo-scientific knowledge.

The irrelevance of all orthodoxies has become increasingly evident in a world which, although torn by civil war, is now manifestly one. The existence of separate churches is a menace to peace and good will. We must have the Church Universal; and that goal can be reached, not through the victory of a single sect, but through a converging evolution that will transcend them all.

It is hard for us to admit that the faith of our ancestors is not destined to conquer the world: we alone are in possession of the truth, and the truth is one. Yet we have to accept the fact that nominal Christians are but a minority on this earth, and believing Christians a minority of that minority. Only half a century ago, it looked as though the world was on the eve of being Europeanized, and as a consequence Christianized, through the overwhelming superiority of the West in material wealth and armaments. That dream, which certainly was not a beautiful dream, has faded away, and cannot be revived. Neither politically nor religiously will the West be able to impose its patterns. The sects will remain with us for centuries; they may even survive indefinitely, as sentimental memories. But the sectarian spirit is evil, and must be combated. Any sect that pretends to be the sole custodian of the truth is a stumbling block in the path of true religion; and, from the point of view of the Church Universal, the Roman Church, far from being truly "Catholic," is only the most rigidly disciplined of the sects.

Free thinkers have constantly been told: "Why disturb earnest and simple souls in the possession of a faith which brings them comfort and impels them to do good?" I certainly have no desire to spread free thought by forcible means; but I want free thinkers not to be half-ashamed of their own convictions. And I challenge both the arguments that are advanced in defense of the sects. I am by no means certain that the churches are invariably a source of comfort: in many cases, they spread, rather than dispel, anguish. "Quietism," repose in God, peace of mind, peace of soul, is a heresy condemned by the church. The orthodox conception of life, in medieval times, in Calvinism, in Pascal and the Jansenists, in Kierkegaard, in Unamuno, in Léon Bloy, in Kafka, in Niebuhr, is tragic: this world a vale of tears, every joy a snare, an angry God, the uncertainty of salvation, the small number of the elect, an eternity of torture. Christianity is not for a contented herd. The church is engaged in a perpetual battle. For every soul, the issue is dubious. Even for the whole army, victory is remote. From these ancestral fears, still potent today, free thought is a liberation.

And I am by no means certain that the churches, throughout history, have been an unmitigated power for good. For orthodoxy implies intolerance: if you have been entrusted with a truth which is the sole key to human salvation, it is your duty to impose that truth; and certainly to extirpate error, through the sword and the stake if need be, as a foul disease. Why should we blush to mention the obvious: the Inquisition, the massacre of the Albigensians and the Waldensians, the holocausts in Spanish America, the wars in the wake of the Reformation, among the fiercest in history? And the evil is not eradicated even in our days. There was a burning sectarian element on both sides of the Spanish Civil War; there is a religious aspect to Anti-Semitism; the world has not yet taken full count of the fearful loss of life that marked the secession of Pakistan, which was inspired by a religious motive. Today, many pure and gentle souls bar out, on religious grounds, any thought of reconciliation with the Soviets: without confessing it to themselves, they are warmongers doing lip service to the Prince of Peace. *Tantum religio potuit suadere malorum*: the line of Lucretius has not lost its bitter truth.

Less lurid, but more pervasive, are two other dangers of the sectarian spirit. The first is the linking of orthodoxy with conservatism. At the origin of the best known religions, there was a violent break with the past. Conversion is a rebellion, a daring adventure; and that can be seen today with neophytes, among us or in distant lands. But for the vast majority, religion is a tradition, or, literally, a prejudice. It is rooted in the dim and hallowed past; it is "the good old religion," the religion we learned at our mother's knees, the faith of our ancestors. So all challenges to the "wisdom of prejudice" seem almost equally sacrilegious. In many cases, it is difficult to tell whether men are political conservatives because they are orthodox, or orthodox because they are conservatives: education, temperament, and interests work in close harmony. Outstanding exceptions were Gladstone and Bryan, who stood at the same time for political radicalism and the strictest fundamentalism in religious belief. As a rule, it is not Holy Writ alone that is "the impregnable rock," but the whole established order; and free thinkers in every domain are equally branded as subversive. Now, I am convinced that our civilization is at present in desperate need of swift, sweeping, intelligent adjustment: else a cataclysm is inevitable. To use again a well-worn simile, it is perilous that the pilot, while shooting the rapids, should be looking obstinately backward. In so far as the churches discourage dynamic free thought, they are hampering our effort to avert revolution.

The other danger, deeper and more insidious still, is that of Pharisaism: self-righteousness founded on orthodox beliefs and practices. This leads to a hopeless distortion of moral values. A man must be wrong, even though his deeds be right, if he cannot recite our articles of faith and does not observe our ritual. The word *libertinism* which at first meant free thought, was twisted to signify *debauchery*. Thomas Paine was dismissed as "a dirty little atheist." On the other hand, those who scrupulously repeat the right words and make the right gestures must be right, though their sins be as scarlet. Gregory of Tours, a saintly bishop, relating the many crimes of the barbarian Clovis, said that he walked before the Lord and did that which was pleasing in His sight. The same praise was bestowed on Marshal Pétain, "a fine Christian gentleman," and on Caudillo Franco, "that man of God." The result is the most naïve and the most noxious self-righteousness in nations, classes, and individuals. Greed is condemned in the gospel: but how could predatory wealth be sinful, when the men who seek it have the right belief, and therefore are good? So, with no malice prepense, the gospel of the poor serves as a bastion for the rich. I am persuaded that many men of high intelligence and undoubted rectitude would be more critical of the injustices by which they profit, if their conscience had not been drugged with orthodoxy.

Be sure that this was not a pleasant chapter to write. But I am committed to free thought, and thought cannot live half slave half free. I know the enormous stream of elaborate thinking that has been poured into Christian theology: I respect the magnitude of the effort, and I deplore the waste. I also know the vast amount of charitable work done by the churches: but a definite social policy would remove the necessity for such charity. I know that most ministers and many of the faithful are hungering for righteousness: but how much more effective would their striving be, if their minds were not shackled! Again, my one desire is not to stifle the religious spirit, but to release it from bondage.

NOTE

This chapter was just completed, when I came across the statement of the Dwight Harrington Terry Foundation (*Lectures on Religion in the Light of Science and Philosophy*, Yale University): "the object is . . . the building of the truths of science and philosophy into the structure of a broadened and purified religion. . . The lectures shall be subject to no philosophical or religious test, and no one who is an earnest seeker after truth shall be excluded because his views seem radical or destructive of existing beliefs. The founder realizes that the liberalism of one generation is often conservatism in the next, and that many an apostle of true liberty has suffered martyrdom at the hands of the orthodox. . . The cardinal principles of the Foundation . . . are loyalty to the truth, lead where it will, and devotion to human welfare."

To this statement I unreservedly subscribe; and I claim that I have been guided by its spirit. It seems to me to express the "orthodoxy" of modern America, our firm common belief. The narrower creeds are sectarian, and might be called "heretical." I wish the chapels of all free universities could be conducted strictly on those lines. At present, the one great rule is not to give offense: the result is not seldom hypocrisy, and at best tepidity. Religion, free from sectarian trammels, should be the core of university teaching; not, as at present, a distant relation whose Sunday visits are endured with frigid courtesy.

CHAPTER XIII

What I believe

Not the void, but the dark . . .

The moment has come to sum up the argument and venture a conclusion. I closed my first book, *French Prophets of Yesterday*, with Renan's anxious words: "What shall they live by, who come after us?" I am now attempting to meet the challenge, which has never been out of my mind for these forty years.

I

Thought is the whole dignity of man, and the sole warrant of his very existence. Yet we cannot be saved merely by taking thought. Science is but diligent and scrupulous rationalism: it collects the facts, and organizes them into intelligible and workable patterns which we call laws. But as Rabelais, Renan, and Aldous Huxley prophesied, science without conscience could turn this earth into a most efficient hell. A rationalist within reason, I feel certain, with the full force of Cartesian *évidence*, that the key to our existence lies beyond human reason.

Art escapes from the bournes of mere intellect, on the wings of imagination and passion. Art the untamable promises salvation from the drabness of a mechanistic Utopia. Art is not the enemy of thought: what art explores, reason may ploddingly conquer, and *reduce* to discipline. But the magic of art is only the willing suspension of disbelief. If a man's soul cannot live by the mere algebra of thought, neither can it be sustained by the insubstantial pageantry of art. Reality lies still beyond.

The first two parts of this book, therefore, point to the necessity of faith, "the substance of things hoped for, the evidence of things not seen." Here comes the third and most perilous temptation. We all yearn to clothe our faith with words and ideas. We dread the abyss between our boundless desire and our sober earthly duties. We send our symbols flying into the immeasurable void, hoping that they will return to us, transmuted into revelations. All this seems to me poetry, primitive and sublime: myths which are but the reaffirmation of our problems and the echoes of our anguish; human thoughts, human words; not an answer from the Eternal Silence.

So I challenge the mythologies which usurp the name of religion. Far from guiding our steps aright, they stand in the way of real religious thought and real religious action. For the unceasing quest which alone is spiritual life, for the mystery around us and within us which literally is *the sacred*, they substitute deceptive certainties, pseudo-historical, pseudo-scientific data, arranged into cut-and-dried metaphysical schemes. And to conceal the vagueness and inaccuracy of the data, the thin rigidity of the systems, the mythologies throw over them the magical and illusory mantle of art: *credo quia pulchrum*.

By religious action, I mean with Jesus the deeds of the good Samaritan: relieving human suffering, and curbing the evils which are its sources. In definite terms, this implies today working for peace, social welfare, and social justice. The sects do lip-service to this ideal. And more than lip-service: they do attempt to alleviate human distress. But their professed, their essential purpose is to expound and maintain a doctrine. If it were not so, they would disappear as sects, and merge into the Church Universal, the fighting conscience of mankind.

As a result, they fail to take the lead against what Renan already called, three quarters of a century ago, *practical atheism*. They do not effectively challenge the materialism, the cynicism, which are manifested in the thirst for power and in the profit motive. They all too readily compromise with those who, in the name of *realism*, affirm that evil is a safer bet than good. If the profiteers adopt the respectable shibboleths, they are held justified, and their standing as church members is not questioned. To affirm that Christ is the only-begotten Son of God is the sole decisive test. A community in which even ministers of the gospel will pour ridicule on "idealists," "perfectionists," and "do-gooders" is one whose light is darkness.

But our minds are conditioned by the traditions of ages. The sects, with their dogmas and their rituals, have claimed sole possession of the religious spirit, as at one time the dynasties claimed to be the sole embodiment of the community spirit. On the face of it, the claims are not wholly unjustified. There *is* religion in the sects: it is their *raison d'être*. They hamper it, but they cannot stifle it altogether. Ardent souls have joined the sects, because there seemed to be no other channel for their spiritual needs. In the same way, men with a delicate conscience have supported tyrannies, because even a tyranny is a government, that is to say an association for the common good, and better than chaos. Apostles of liberty have volunteered for military service, although they knew that army life is slavery undisguised, because at that particular time the army appeared as a sword in the hand of freedom.

Need I repeat that I feel the greatest sympathy for the earnest members of the sects? My closest friends are among them: we commune in the depths of our souls. I do not blame those men who revere tradition, conform to custom, collaborate with the established authorities. My own temperament is extremely, I should say excessively, conservative: I am not sure that in the France of 1942 I should have taken to the *Maquis*. Least of all do I desire to stir up religious strife. The issue of sect or no sect does not present itself to us with the tragic urgency of a civil war. There is a tradition of free thought in the West, which goes back at least as far as the Renaissance, and perhaps as far as Abélard. Freedom of thought is the rule of our universities, and is guaranteed by our Constitution.[1] My own ex-

---

[1] We are not quite sure whether this is officially a Christian country: the Covenanters think it is not, and for that reason refuse, with courageous logic, to acknowledge our government as legitimate. Several Jews have sat in the Supreme Court. There was no objection to President W. H. Taft on the score of his being a Unitarian; and certainly Washington, Jefferson, and Lincoln, whose shrines are so conspicuous in our national capital, could not be called Fundamentalists. On the other hand, in San Francisco, a Humanist Society was denied the use of the radio, as nontheistic.

perience has been smooth and pleasant enough. I made my
independent position perfectly clear in my first book, and it has
never created for me the shadow of a difficulty. So I do not have
to urge a rebellion against the thrall of orthodoxy: a shrug
suffices. The fight against the ghosts is entirely within. I wish
at times there were Dagons to defy. The confused blend of
superstitions, irrational logic, sentiment, and conventional art
offers a viscid, tenacious, almost invincible obstacle to honest
thought and determined action. The sects will oppose to their
dying day the purification of religion from these parasitical
growths: infirm of faith, they fear that they might be purified
out of existence

II

The fight against my own ghosts has been over for so long
that I can hardly recall it: for, it was rightly said, nothing is so
tenuous as a ghost once you no longer believe in it. It may be
that to some I shall appear as a Peter Schlemihl: only the Devil
could so neatly remove your shadow. The fear of death never
tormented me. Among the most sincere poems of my adolescence, there are a few which express a longing for death. Before
I had read Baudelaire, I could have cried, at rare but impas-
sioned moments:

> O Death, old Captain! It is time; let us weigh anchor.
> This country is boring us, O Death! Let us set sail . . .

Throughout the long years, I could face without flinching the
thought that I might cease to be; and the thought has no terror
now that the hour is near. Call this stoicism or Christian resignation: it is not the name that matters, but the equanimity. I
am here with definite tasks to perform, and definite opportunities for enjoyment: I too "accept the Universe." But I do not
rebel at the possibility that tomorrow I may be transferred to
some other sphere, or allowed to rest for ever.

Among the few dogmas that I reject outright, scorning even
a casual discussion, is the belief in eternal punishment, meted
out by an all-good and all-powerful god. It seems to me a sadis-

tic (or masochistic) nightmare. We all have moments of impotent rage: "Oh that my enemy were in my power!"; and even in the twentieth century, men have relished torture as a fine art. It is this craving for inflicting pain (there is a faint trace of it in our enjoyment of the noblest tragedy) that we objectify as the Moloch of an avenging God. This craving belongs to our lowest nature, which is not our deepest. For I hold that the unconscious and the subconscious are peripheral and shallow; our truest self is the one revealed by our intelligence and controlled by our will.

So the fear of death and the fear of hell are so faint within me that I doubt whether I ever felt them in my heart: I have only been told about them. The hope of eternal bliss is perhaps even fainter. It is a commonplace that no sect has ever been able to make heaven attractive, or even convincing. A materialistic heaven of eternal revelry is an appalling thought. An everlasting concert of sacred music is merely a dull metaphor. To see the glory of God face to face is absurd, for the Infinite has no face. The only logical conception is resorption into the Absolute, when the flaw we call existence has been purged away. But that is Nirvana, not immortality.

The idea of personal survival seems to me exceedingly naïve. The resurrection of our actual bodies would demand a material earth under our material feet, and material food for our restored organs. If we reject this as crude, if we are to be freed from the limitations of our senses, what remains of our personality? I feel certain that thought is not a mere secretion of matter: but our earthly selves are linked with the flesh wherein they dwell. What confines us, defines us: liberated, we cease to exist. Transmigration is more acceptable than bodily resurrection; but if an abstract principle within me survives, entirely cut off from my blood, my impressions, my sensations, my memories, my language, my knowledge: what will this purified being or this new avatar have in common with my present personality? I am no hero: I have known fear. Fear is the reasonable realization of danger: if a man has to walk across a stream on a rotten plank, he would be a fool not to know that the plank may break. I fear accidents; I fear disease; I fear infirmities; I fear most of all the humiliating loss of vigor entailed by age. But I do not fear death.

Beyond fear is dread: faceless, nameless, physiological. Our duty is to challenge dread, and reduce it to reasonable fear. Often the gigantic shadow will vanish altogether; or it may be identified with a definite peril which, if it cannot be warded off, must be faced with open eyes. Collective dread is panic, which takes hold of herds, human or animal, and hurls them into demented flight: nations are panicked into wars. Half way between fear and dread stands anguish: man tries vaguely to reason out the causes of his obscure dismay; and he reaches the anthropomorphic hypothesis that he is in the hands of a hidden and implacable power. This mysterious enemy he dare not defy or accuse: like a whipped cur, he accepts punishment as evidence of guilt. But the guilt, thus forced upon him, remains undefined, and cannot be atoned for. This is the unfathomable dread moralized, not rationalized, by Kierkegaard and Kafka: we are on trial, but we know not before what judge, nor for what offense, nor in virtue of what law. To escape from this oppressive sense of guilt, there is no opiate that man is not ready to swallow.

I have no such feeling of undefined guilt attaching to the whole human race. The idea that existence, per se, is the original sin, and that Nirvana alone can restore purity, is too abstract for my Western mind. If there be guilt on the cosmic plane, it rests with the Creator, not with the helpless toys he made for his own amusement or "glory." If we are under a curse, cursèd be that curse! On the human plane, I do believe in collective remorse. Vigny, whenever he met a woman, felt he ought to crave her pardon. Racial supremacy is a sin, and the day of atonement is still far off. If we felt our responsibility intensely enough, that sin could be washed away even from our deepest South. Wealth is a sin, so long as destitution exists. All sensitive souls are conscious that they are enjoying ill-gotten advantages, which inflict upon others humiliation or distress; and like Tolstoy until the last few weeks of his life, they cannot find a clear path to renunciation and purification. This sense of guilt is our noblest attribute; it is the divine discontent which raises us above the brutish level. Directed into the proper channels, it would wipe away obvious ills, and constantly discover deeper ones, for it can never lead us into a static Utopia. It is the *Deus vult!* of the eternal crusade. Here the sects force themselves in. They screen and blur that healthy sense of responsibility with the myth of the Fall, and they offer to heal our uneasy conscience with a metaphysical nostrum.

I am fully conscious of individual sin also: not merely of the triple curse of being a male, a white man, and a *bourgeois*. I am what is conventionally known as a *good* man: I have kept the vows of poverty, obedience, and chastity imposed upon the academic clergy. Like Joseph de Maistre, when I probe the conscience of an honest man — myself — I shudder. I am not alluding to mere *faux pas* due to errors of judgment: these cause regrets, not remorse. Maladjustment, and the clumsy efforts to correct it, are the chief sources of sin. My peace with society is an uneasy truce; my inner peace is even more precarious. Worst of the sins due to maladjustment is compromise; the open, degrading lie, and the equivocation which is morally a lie, both the result of cowardice. In the murk beyond that uneasy twilight, I find the survival of animal impulses in defiance of reason. I shall never be weary of repeating that I am no Rousseauist: primitivism is not goodness, nor innocence, nor even irresponsibility, it is blindness. These impulses are fierce, not deep; but because they are wild, cool reason is too equable to meet their sudden and violent impact. Let the tamer relax his vigilance, or lose faith in his own mastery, and the beast is upon him. The chief manifestations of these impulses are anger and jealousy. Both were ascribed to God Himself: the Bible speaks of a jealous God, and Jonathan Edwards of an angry God.

III

There are metaphysical questions which do not exist on the moral or practical plane; and I need not repeat my opinion of metaphysics. Metaphysically, liberty is inconceivable. An eternal, omniscient, omnipotent Providence leaves absolutely no room for human freedom. Beyond quibbling, whatever is foreseen is foreordained, and God can not be surprised and shocked at our antics. The scientific-metaphysical conception of absolute and eternal law likewise destroys the possibility of an autonomous human will: here predestination is called determinism. If the universe is an infinite faultless mechanism, in which every cause is inevitably followed by its effect, the God of Cybernetics could plot out in every detail the course of an individual life, as infallibly as an astronomer can tell where Saturn will be on the fifteenth of March 1984. All this is irrefutable, and self-refuting. Let liberty be the merest *as if*, no moral life is conceivable without it. Let its domain be encroached upon by all the sciences of nature and of man, particularly physiology, psychology and anthropology, it is also constantly expanding. The race between determinism and liberty will last to the end of time. It may end this very minute, if I should suddenly wake up in a different universe.

In the same way, the controversy about progress leaves me indifferent. Again from the theologico-metaphysical point of view, there can be no progress. From the material point of view, I admit that of the developments we commonly call progress not a single one is inevitable, not a single one is irreversible, not a single one is necessarily good. We are told that the improvement in our plumbing is blurring our sense of moral values: I doubt whether a return to primitive simplicity would greatly help our souls. My conception of progress is not "two helicopters in every garage," or "every salesman a Ph.D." But my ultimate faith is that there is some *sense* to this universe: the word is intentionally vaguer than *purpose* or *meaning*. Whatever works *with* that sense is progress. Reinhold Niebuhr, who a generation after Georges Sorel, two centuries after Rousseau, is pouring contempt on the delusions of progress, still is an inveterate servant of the good. He is fighting manifest evils in the hope of attaining a larger degree of justice and charity. If progress be an absurdity, then all his activities are in vain.

The metaphysical objections to progress in the abstract are camouflaged defenses against definite steps forward. Vested interests (including the theologies) maintain that no progress is possible — except of course their own expansion.

I am not expounding a system: I cannot start from a single assumption. I can not go beyond Descartes: unable to doubt my own doubt, I am compelled to assert my own existence. But, if we by-pass solipsism as barren, the ego is at once entangled with the non-ego, the clear with the dim; and beyond the dim, the unknown; and all through, pervading even the very core of the ego, the mystery. This, I admit, is a romantic view of life, as remote as possible from the luminous rationalism of the classic mind.

IV

What is my starting point? Probably self-respect, which is a form of self-love, which is a form of self-assertion. I have to live with my Self, and I want to be in decent company. So the first and simplest commandment is: "Act in such a way that thou shalt not have to despise thyself." In theological language: "Do not debase the image of God." Contempt is more devastating than hatred: hatred may be coupled with reluctant admiration, and may suddenly be transmuted into love. The common butt of all contempt is cowardice. Fear we must acknowledge and measure and combat: but we should never yield to fear; and we should scorn those who seek to impose their will through fear. Fear of course is not purely physical: physical cowardice is the most excusable of all. Fear of poverty; fear of isolation; fear of not standing well with the many or with the successful few: when these fears paralyze thought and warp action, they become deadly sins. Cowardice means slavery, and the moral life demands freedom. Franklin Roosevelt was right when he so insisted upon freedom from fear. That freedom is not merely one of four, it is the ultimate citadel, and its name is self-respect. We should be ready to face want, rather than submit to fear; and nothing can abridge our freedom of thought, except our own fear.

Freedom, however, is merely a condition: adopted as a guide, it might prove misleading. In childhood and youth, I have rebelled against disciplines which I accepted at heart, simply because they were imposed: futile revolt is not freedom. What is now my criterion? Act in harmony with the *sense* of the universe. That there is such a sense must be accepted on faith; it is the very essence of faith. When many thinkers down to Albert Camus proclaimed that the world was *absurd* (had no *sense*), they were fighting absurdity by denouncing it; they were not absurd in their own hearts. Those who hold that we may deliberately turn our back upon such a faith in order to be *realistic*, are, I must repeat after Renan, the true, the militant atheists.

How is that sense revealed to us, if we discard the books and traditions of the innumerable conflicting sects? The compass turns to the magnetic North; Descartes believed that good sense, imparted to all men, enabled us to discern the truth; innumerable teachers, Rousseau and Kant the most explicit, hold that such a moral compass exists, and is called conscience. Broadly, I agree with them: the moral law in our hearts, the categorical imperative, is our sole inspiration. If the term be used symbolically, not dogmatically, I should be glad to call it the voice of God within us.

But man is not a pure spirit: he is conditioned by his body of flesh, and the bodies of his ancestors still alive in him, and the vague enormous mass of their traditions, and the influence of his fellow-men. So the voice of his conscience, although it may seem direct and simple, is the complex result of a long evolution. Carlyle among others attempted to draw a distinction between *honor*, a collective code, transmitted, imposed, and *conscience*, the immediate response of the individual soul. Honor in the Carlylean sense (which is not Vigny's) is in many cases mere perversity with aristocratic prestige. A lawyer, a financier, a diplomat, a politician, are allowed by their professional code to lie, and even to glory in deception: Bismarck gloated over his shabby tricks, and yet he was a man of honor. A gentleman of the old school could not engage in any gainful occupation: parasitism was the cornerstone of his code. For him to defraud his commercial creditors was a peccadillo; but his gambling debts must be punctiliously settled. He might steal his friend's wife, if he were ready to give satisfaction by killing the husband in *honorable* duel. The crimes perpetrated to vindicate the "honor" of national flags outweigh the murders committed by professional bandits.

But the conscience of the common man, although freer from *noblesse oblige* distortion, is likewise a historical and a social product: a set of loyalties, a code of honor. In order to become reliable, conscience should be stripped of all prejudices of race, caste, party, nation, or sect. Otherwise, it is not the individual soul that responds, but, say, the German way of life with which that soul is wrapped. That stripping is a delicate process: can it ever reach a definite end? If we peel off, one after another, the layers of prejudice that surround a conscience, are we certain that we shall find a core? Pascal was right: "They say habit is a second nature: what if nature were but a first habit?"

Traditions, superstitions, philosophies, and art itself build only bridges of phantasmagoria between the Mystery and our earthly labor. There are men who believe that they have spanned the chasm: the mystics. In ecstasy they feel the oneness between their own life and the life universal. The rationalist has no right to deny *a priori* the possibility and the validity of such an experience, which by definition is beyond his scope. The case for the mystic vision is not weakened by the fact that it may be linked with conflicting creeds: there are mystics in all faiths, among Buddhists and Mohammedans as well as among Christians. This proves only the infirmity of human speech and the irrelevance of historical dogmas. Nor is the evidence finally disposed of, because, in a number of cases, there is legitimate suspicion that it is not genuine. Charlatans do not destroy the validity of science, nor do false witnesses invalidate the whole of history. Mystery and mystification come close together; so do the fakir and the faker. From the desire to know arises the will to believe ("Lord, I believe; help thou mine unbelief"); and at that point, the will to make-believe be-

comes an ever-present danger. Ardent prayer, a spiritual tragedy which we play in the depths of our souls, reaches its catharsis, which we accept as a response. Psychical research may
help us weed out deliberate swindles and the more obvious
cases of self-delusion. But I do not see how the most searching
psychology could ever hope to understand ecstasy, which is too
evidently beyond learning and wisdom. I have seen rapt faces
among the Indians thronging in the Guadalupe shrine: they
were soaring into spheres where Georges Dumas and William
James would have been unable to follow.

In human terms, this experience *means* nothing, *proves*
nothing. For the individual, it may have the force of Cartesian
self-evidence. But it is incommunicable, and valid only for the
soul whom it ravishes: mysticism at secondhand is nonsense,
mysticism in twenty lessons is a hoax. It seems a scandal that
a revelation of such commanding value should be granted to
so few. Why should not God speak to all His children?

It might be that the mystic sense, now so rare and so capri-
ciously distributed, is growing imperceptibly throughout mankind, as language and the reasoning power once did. We can
easily imagine, in remote ages, men centuries ahead of their
fellows attempting to express themselves in ways beyond the
reach of the herd. They would, in obscure fashion, be put
down as odd or even mad; they might also be looked upon with
awe and reverence, although their half-articulate message remained cryptic. In the course of aeons, *all* men were taught to
think and to speak: children of three now master the instrument for which the geniuses of the pre-eolithic age groped so
clumsily. Perhaps there are among us, and have been for the
few thousand years of recorded history, pioneers of a new
stage, stray units of a humanity in process of transcending
reason, as once did reason transcend instinct. I do not *know*:
but I want to keep my mind, and more than my mind, "all that
is within me," open for the promise of such a promotion. Of
one thing I am certain: I might prepare my soul for such a
light by repeating the Beatitudes, or St. Paul's great hymn to
charity; but never by reaffirming Leviticus and Deuteronomy,

the Athanasian Creed, the Westminster Catechism, or the Thirty-nine Articles. These do not point the way: they padlock the gate.

But, whether you think in terms of a grace parsimoniously imparted from above, or of a seed growing through the whole of mankind, the mystic experience, in its full directness and intensity, is rare in our days, and it is uncertain. Not only are ordinary mortals skeptical about such a transcendental gift, but the favored ones themselves have their hours of doubt and despair. The reason is perhaps that the pure beatific vision was linked in their minds with definite events, institutions, ideas. There come hours of disenchanted soberness in which the discrepancy between vision and reality becomes torturingly manifest. When Joan of Arc met the Dauphin, she must have been sorely tempted to doubt the divine character of her mission. No blinding illumination has ever come to me. Among the leaders whom I revere, Pascal alone was a mystic in the full meaning of the term: yet he too had to resort to desperate remedies: the wager, the opiate. Hugo was a seer, but a seer is half a poet, that is to say, an artist: he induces visions and rejoices in them. At best, he can only suspend disbelief.

In this loftier sphere, I am inclined to adopt the hypothesis that I have already discussed in the realms of reason and of art. Like Descartes's *good sense*, like the aesthetic response, *mysticism is universal*. Every man, at some moment of his existence, be it ever so humble, or, far worse, be it ever so hectic, has felt its irresistible power. But we feel it in utter darkness. The ineffable imposes silence. It cannot be comprehended, it cannot be remembered, it leaves no intelligible trace. There remains with us only an undefinable longing for a truth, for a peace, for a love passing all understanding. Metaphysics, theology, by rational means; ritual, by material ones, are attempts to end the quest. What they offer is but a painted screen, a *trompe-l'œil* claiming to be the ultimate reality. Art is the quest for the lost glimpse of a more real world: but we know that it never is quite true.

A common man may never have known ecstasy, and yet have

his share of the mystic sense. Ecstasy is but a paroxysm: the mystic sense pervading the whole of existence is what I call faith: congruency with the unutterable, oneness with the *sense* of life. There is more faith diffused through the whole of mankind than in the rare and magnificent flashes of the professed mystics. Seers, poets, and conquerors are portents: we are awed by their unique power. But spiritual life is not made up of portents: it is an obscure and constant endeavor.

"And, behold, the Lord passed by, and a great and strong wind rent the mountains, and brake in pieces the rocks before the Lord; but the Lord was not in the wind: and after the wind an earthquake; but the Lord was not in the earthquake: and after the earthquake a fire; but the Lord was not in the fire: and after the fire a still small voice."

V

Before the voice — so still, so small in the tumult of the world — can reach our ears, there must be a desire to listen. That desire is confusedly blended with historical and social elements: these must be hushed, or they will deafen us to the voice. Our first duty then is to purify our sense of duty. This is what I mean — the formula, with variations, will be found many times in my writings — by *good will and the critical spirit*. Goodness is futile without *will*; good will itself, i.e., will at the service of the good, may be blind and harmful if not checked by clear thinking and dispassionate inquiry. But nothing is so barren as mere analysis. The critical spirit, in absolute purity, *stets verneint*, ever denies. Fact-finding will not point the way, unless you know first where you want to go.

"Where I want to go" is what I call the good. It is not identical with the true. For whatever is, is true: diseases are facts, and so are sins. The quest for the good implies a selection. Again, we must "take things as they are": that is pure science. We must not leave them as they are: government, poetry, religion, are efforts to order the facts so as to achieve our desire. Science is an inventory; religion is a campaign.

I cannot accept the Machiavellian antinomy between "the

good" and "interests." Nothing is good that works to the detriment of mankind. The distinction is purely one of perspective: the narrow *vs.* the far-sighted. It is to a man's *interest*, i.e., it gives him satisfaction, to drink his fill: but beware of the ignoble nemesis. It is to a man's interest, if he happen to be strong, determined and lazy, to plunder his timid and hardworking neighbor: but a land of banditry is less rich and less happy, even for the bandits, than one that is well policed. It is to the immediate interest of man or nation to play fast and loose with engagements: say, to make Trieste a free state, and then offer it as a bait to Italy. But it is this Bismarckian kind of cleverness that has kept Europe at war for centuries. What we call *the good* is the sum total of long-range general interests (I prefer to avoid such terms as *permanent* and *universal*). What we call realism is the defense of immediate and special interests. In the larger frame, realism is self-defeating. It is, for instance, extremely unrealistic of the French not to liquidate their empire: if still possible by transforming it into a genuine democratic union. The interests they are so stubbornly defending are those of a few colonists, a few investors, a few officials and officers. Over their pettiness is thrown the purple cloak of national honor: an honor rooted in conquest, which is dishonor. It is unrealistic for business leaders to fight for the right of amassing millions: by so doing they perpetuate in all nations a latent civil war. If they were devoting their energy and ability to the creation of an intelligent welfare state, they would save us decades of snarling confusion, perhaps a violent upheaval, and its inevitable sequel, years of ruthless dictatorship.

All this might sound like orthodox Utilitarianism: the greatest good of the greatest number over the longest period of time. The formula is clumsy: an accumulation of superlatives is meaningless. Then it is question-begging: why should *I* sacrifice myself to the mass or to posterity? I am certain that I am I; I am far less certain that I am a cell in a vast organism. It happens that in my own case, my personal interests and those of the community do not clash. But if I had a chance to acquire slaves, grab natural resources, corner a necessity of life, would I be able to withstand the temptation? Utilitarianism, which is but enlightened selfishness, can never justify the sacrifice of the individual: it is most unrealistic for a man to offer his life in Korea.

My initial principle: I must preserve my self-respect, is not an infallible guide. If my test is: *Ne pas être un salaud*, not to be a profiteer; the profiteer, quite as honestly, might adopt as a rule of life: Not to be a sucker. He would despise himself if he saw a good thing and failed to grab it. Grope as I may, I cannot get hold of a definite principle that can be stated in intellectual terms. I am inexorably driven to *faith*, the substance of things hoped for. So, again, I believe — against what accumulation of realistic evidence! — that there is a *sense* in this universe. When my awareness of this sense is blurred, I feel lost and unhappy. When I am conscious of straining against that sense, I am assailed by remorse and despair. Moments of plenitude, peace, and joy were rare in my life, and may have been delusive; still they sufficed to steady my faith.

Why do I insist upon using the vague metaphor: "there is a *sense* in this universe," when the time-honored terms *God* and *Love* are ready to hand? I am conscious of the wealth of sacred associations that they possess; conscious also that by rejecting them, I am giving offense to many who are active in the good fight. But I am even more conscious of the confusions that these words create; and I cannot shirk the duty of denouncing these confusions.

The word *God* evokes both the Metaphysical Absolute, a pretentious vestment for the inconceivable, and the Fighting God, a splendid metaphor, but frankly anthropomorphic, fraught with contradictions, and linked with tribal legends. My guide must be more of a living force than the God of the Philosophers; more of a mystery than the God of Abraham.

I am reluctant to call my ultimate principle *love*: "one word is too often profaned for me to profane it." It is difficult to soar beyond the commonplace: "it is love, it is love, that makes the world go round." A dispassionate analysis destroys the immediacy of the experience: the result is pedantry or cynicism. I admire La Rochefoucauld, Stendhal, and Proust, yet I feel that they lead away from the core of the problem. Sentimental effusions are far worse: they are particularly repellent to me, even in Michelet, who was a great soul.

My essential objection to the word *love* is that we inevitably link it with *sex* and with *jealousy*, two turbid forces alien to the Power I am seeking. I resent the identification of love with sex. The erotic imagery of certain mystics has no appeal to me. The glowing sensuality of the Song of Songs has the purity of fire: but to turn it into a theological symbol seems to me arrant blasphemy. Lust exists in the brutes, and in the human brute too, in the form of whoring, without a particle of what I would recognize as love. And love can be completely divorced from sex. A dog and I loved each other for sixteen years; I feel we are mingled still, "he half alive, and I half dead." I do not want to minimize the power and the beauty of sheer physical attraction: a blind instinct which we may dignify by the name of vital urge. I admit that it is possible for sex, companionship, and love to unite: blending, they create a force which has no equal in our existence, just as charcoal, sulphur, and saltpeter combined have a power not found in the separate elements.

In the higher animals, and in man, we find possessiveness, or jealousy. It is assumed that love justifies jealousy, is inseparable from jealousy. Yet we know that possessiveness is not good. It is the most outrageous expansion of the ego, seeking to impose its will upon another creature. The person owned becomes an object, a piece of property, and ceases to be a free agent. The selfishness, the cruelty, are not redeemed because they are mutual. The jail remains a jail, even when both prisoners are also jailers.

Sectarian religion and patriotism have made jealousy a virtue: a nation is a jealous god. Is it possible to purify the idea of love from the curse of possessiveness? In many fields, this is not inconceivable. Our ultimate loyalty is only to the highest: I cannot give unconditional allegiance to sect, party, country, "right or wrong." Love for a faith, a land, a cause, can be ardent and holy without being exclusive. I love all the countries I have known at first hand, France, England, Germany, America, Morocco, Mexico. I can feel love for the spirit of all religions, and even rejoice in the quaintness of their historical garments. I can love all great causes, particularly liberty *and* social justice. And this means that I do not, that I cannot, *belong* to any one of them.

If a word be needed, let us seek one that is unsullied; and, beyond words, let us strive to voice the ineffable through solemn music. That is why, rejecting systems, legends, hierarchies, and rituals, I feel I may close with the great lyric notes of St. Paul, in the thirteenth chapter of his First Epistle to the Corinthians:

"Though I speak with the tongues of men and angels, and have not charity, I am become as sounding brass, or a tinkling cymbal. And though I have the gift of prophecy, and understand all mysteries, and all knowledge; and though I have all faith, so that I could remove mountains, and have not charity, I am nothing. And though I bestow all my goods to feed the poor, and though I give my body to be burned, and have not charity, it profiteth me nothing. Charity suffereth long, and is kind; charity envieth not; charity vaunteth not itself, is not puffed up, doth not behave itself unseemly, seeketh not her own, is not easily provoked, thinketh no evil; rejoiceth not in iniquity, but rejoiceth in the truth; beareth all things, believeth all things, hopeth all things, endureth all things. Charity never faileth: but whether there be prophecies, they shall fail; whether there be tongues, they shall cease; whether there be knowledge, it shall vanish away. For we know in part, and we prophesy in part. But when that which is perfect is come, then that which is in part shall be done away. When I was a child, I spake as a child, I understood as a child, I thought as a child: but when I became a man, I put away childish things. For now we see through a glass, darkly; but then face to face: now I know in part; but then shall I know even as also I am known. And now abideth faith, hope and charity, these three; but the greatest of these is charity."

EPILOGUE

Proverbs of a Humanist

Be a rationalist — within reason.

Be guided by conscious, conscientious good will; but do good with a critical mind.

Gladly suspend disbelief: even make-believe may rise to the dignity of a symbol. But put thy trust in steadfast doubt.

Doubt until thou canst doubt no more. Pause, and resume the course of thy doubt. For doubt is thought, and thought is life. Systems, which end doubt, are devices for drugging thought.

Serve both the Many (through Civilization) and the One (through Culture): work for a highly organized community of philosophical anarchists.

Trust not the wiles of little men: they prevail but for a moment.

Call nothing thy own, except thy soul.

Spurn hatred and fear: they are debasing. And self-contempt is hell on earth.

Have no faith but in faith: which is the hope that charity is not vain.

Love all gods, except a jealous God.

Love Nature and Man, Science and Art: but be ready to see the heavens roll up like a scroll.

Son navire est coulé, sa vie est révolue.
Il jette la bouteille à la mer, et salue
Les jours de l'avenir qui pour lui sont venus.